Bill Bryson was born in 1951 in Des Moines, Iowa, and grew up there. He is a graduate of Drake University and while studying there worked as a copy-editor for the *Des Moines Register*. He has lived in England for several years and has worked for the *Bournemouth Evening Echo*, *Financial Weekly* and, since 1980, *The Times*, where he is a deputy chief sub-editor. He is the author of one other book and has written extensively for newspapers and magazines throughout the English-speaking world. He is married, with two children, and lives in Virginia Water

D0238573

BILL BRYSON

THE PENGUIN DICTIONARY OF
TROUBLESOME WORDS

PENGUIN BOOKS

Penguin Books Ltd, Harmondsworth, Middlesex, England
Viking Penguin Inc., 40 West 23rd Street, New York, New York 10010, U.S.A.
Penguin Books Australia Ltd, Ringwood, Victoria, Australia
Penguin Books Canada Ltd, 2801 John Street, Markham, Ontario, Canada L3R 1B4
Penguin Books (N.Z.) Ltd, 182–190 Wairau Road, Auckland 10, New Zealand

First published 1984
Published simultaneously by Allen Lane
Reprinted 1984 (twice)

Printed in Great Britain by
Richard Clay (The Chaucer Press) Ltd, Bungay, Suffolk
Filmset in Monophoto Times by
Northumberland Press Ltd, Gateshead

CONTENTS

INTRODUCTION

This book might more accurately, if less convincingly, have been called
*A Guide to Everything in English Usage That the Author Wasn't Entirely
Clear About Until Quite Recently*. Much of what follows is the product
of questions encountered during the course of daily newspaper work:
should it be 'fewer than 10 per cent of voters' or 'less than 10 per
cent'? Does someone have 'more money than her' or 'than she'?

The answers to such questions are not always easily found. Seeking
the guidance of colleagues is, I discovered, dangerous: raise almost
any point of usage with two journalists and you will almost certainly
get two confident, but entirely contradictory, answers. Traditional
reference works are often little more helpful because they so frequently
assume from the reader a familiarity with the intricacies of grammar
that is – in my case, at any rate – generous. Once you have said that
in correlative conjunctions in the subjunctive mood there should be
parity between the protasis and apodosis, you have said about all
there is to say on the matter. But you have also, I think, left most
of us as confused as before. I have therefore tried in this book to
use technical terms as sparingly as possible (but have included a
glossary at the end for those that do appear).

For most of us the rules of English grammar are at best a dimly
remembered thing. But even for those who make the rules, grammatical correctitude sometimes proves easier to urge than to achieve.
Among the errors cited in this book are a number committed by some
of the leading authorities of this century. If men such as Fowler and
Bernstein and Quirk and Howard cannot always get their English
right, is it reasonable to expect the rest of us to?

The point is one that has not escaped the notice of many structural
linguists, some of whom regard the conventions of English usage as
intrusive and anachronistic and elitist, the domain of pedants and old
men. In *American Tongue and Cheek*, Jim Quinn, a sympathizer,
savages those who publish 'private lists of language peeves. Professional busybodies and righters of imaginary wrongs, they are the
Sunday visitors of language, dropping in weekly on the local poor
to make sure that everything is up to their own idea of standard ...'
(cited by William Safire in *What's The Good Word?*).

There is no doubt something in what these critics say. Usage authorities can be maddeningly resistant to change, if not actively obstructive. Many of our most seemingly unobjectionable words – precarious, intensify, freakish, mob, banter, brash – had to fight long battles, often lasting a century or more, to gain acceptance. Throughout the nineteenth century reliable was opposed on the dubious grounds that any adjective springing from rely ought to be relionable. Laughable, it was insisted, should be laugh-at-able.

Even now, many good writers scrupulously avoid hopefully and instead write the more cumbersome 'it is hoped' to satisfy an obscure point of grammar, which, I suspect, many of them could not elucidate. Prestigious is still widely avoided in Britain in deference to its nineteenth-century definition, and there remains a large body of users who would, to employ Fowler's words, sooner eat peas with a knife than split an infinitive. Those who sniff decay in every shift of sense or alteration of usage do the language no service. Too often for such people the notion of good English has less to do with expressing ideas clearly than with making words conform to some arbitrary pattern.

But at the same time, anything that helps to bring order to a language as unruly and idiosyncratic as English is almost by definition a good thing. Even the most ardent structuralist would concede that there must be at least some conventions of usage. Otherwise we might as well spell fish (as George Bernard Shaw once wryly suggested) as ghoti: 'gh' as in tough, 'o' as in women, and 'ti' as in motion. By the most modest extension it should be evident that clarity is better served if we agree to preserve a distinction between its and it's, between 'I lay down the law' and 'I lie down to sleep', between imply and infer, forego and forgo, flout and flaunt, anticipate and expect and countless others.

No one, least of all me, has the right to tell you how to organize your words, and there is scarcely an entry in the pages that follow that you may not wish to disregard sometimes and no doubt a few that you may decide to scorn for ever. The purpose of this book is to try to provide a simple guide to the more perplexing or contentious issues of standard written English – or what the American authority John Simon, in an unguarded moment, called the normative grapholect. If you wish to say 'between you and I' or use fulsome in the sense of lavish, you are entirely within your rights and can certainly find ample supporting precedents among many distinguished writers. But you may also find it useful to know that such usages are at variance with that eccentric, ever-shifting corpus known as Good English.

Most of the entries that follow are illustrated with questionable usages from leading British and American newspapers and magazines. I should perhaps hasten to point out that the frequency with which some publications are cited has less to do with the quality of their production than with my own reading habits. *The Times* of London easily appears more often than any other publication, but then it is my job to read *The Times*.

I have also not hesitated to cite errors committed by the authorities themselves. It is, of course, manifestly ungrateful of me to draw attention to the occasional lapses of those on whom I have so unashamedly relied for almost all that I know. My intention in so doing was not to embarrass or challenge them, but simply to show how easily such errors are made, and I hope they will be taken in that light.

It is to those authorities – most especially to Theodore Bernstein, Philip Howard, Sir Ernest Gowers and the incomparable H. W. Fowler – that I am most indebted. I am also deeply grateful to my wife, Cynthia, for her infinite patience; to Donald McFarlan and my father, W. E. Bryson, for their advice and encouragement; to Alan Howe of *The Times* and, not least, to Keith Taylor, who was given the thankless task of editing the manuscript. To all of them, thank you.

A Note on Presentation

To impose a consistent system of presentation in a work of this sort can result in the pages of the book being littered with italics, quotation marks or other typographical devices. Bearing this in mind, I have employed a system that I hope will be easy on the reader's eye as well as easy to follow.

Within each entry, the entry word and any other similarly derived or closely connected words are italicized only when the sense would seem to require it. Other words and phrases – synonyms, antonyms, correct/incorrect alternatives, etc. – are set within quotation marks, but again only when the sense requires it. In both cases, where there is no ambiguity, no typographical device is used to distinguish the word.

a, an. Do you say a hotel or an hotel? A historian or an historian? The convention is to use *a* before an aspirated 'h' (a house, a hotel, a historian) and *an* before a silent 'h'. In this second category there are only four words: hour, heir, honour (US honor) and honest, and their derivatives. Some British authorities allow *an* before hotel and historian, but almost all prefer *a*.

Errors involving *a* and *an* are no doubt more often a consequence of carelessness than of ignorance. They are particularly common when they precede a number, as here: 'Cox will contribute 10 percent of the equity needed to build a $80 million cable system' (*Washington Post*). Make it *an*. Similarly, *a* is unnecessary in the following sentence and should be deleted: 'With a 140 second-hand wide-bodied jets on the market, the enthusiasm to buy anything soon evaporated' (*Sunday Times*).

abdicate, abrogate, abjure, adjure, arrogate, derogate. All six of these words have been confused in a startling variety of ways. Abdicate, the least troublesome of the six, means to renounce or relinquish. Abrogate means to abolish or annul. Abjure means to abstain from, or to reject or retract. Adjure means to command, direct or appeal to earnestly. Arrogate (a close relation of *arrogance*) means to appropriate presumptuously or to assume without right. And derogate (think of *derogatory*) means to belittle.

Those, very baldly, are the meanings. It may help you a little if you remember that the prefix *ab-* indicates 'away from' and *ad-* 'towards'. It might help the rest of us even more, however, if you were to remember that all of these words (with the possible exception of abdicate) have a number of shorter, more readily understood and generally less pretentious synonyms.

abjure. See ABDICATE, ABROGATE, ABJURE, ADJURE, ARROGATE, DEROGATE.

abrogate. See ABDICATE, ABROGATE, ABJURE, ADJURE, ARROGATE, DEROGATE.

accrue does not mean simply to increase in size, but rather to be added to bit by bit. A balloon, for instance, cannot accrue. Except in its legal and financial senses, the word is better avoided.

acoustics. As a science, the word is singular ('Acoustics was his line of work'). As a collection of properties, it is plural ('The acoustics in the auditorium were not good').

acute, chronic. These two are sometimes confused, which is a little puzzling since their meanings are sharply opposed. *Chronic* pertains to lingering conditions, ones that are not easily overcome. *Acute* refers to those that come to a sudden crisis and require immediate attention. People in the Third World may suffer from a chronic shortage of food. In a bad year, their plight may become acute.

adage frequently, and unnecessarily, appears with 'old' in tow. An adage is by definition old.

adjure. See ABDICATE, ABROGATE, ABJURE, ADJURE, ARROGATE, DEROGATE.

admit to is always wrong, as here: 'Pretoria admits to raid against Angola' (*Guardian* headline). Delete *to*. You admit a misdeed, you do not admit to it.

adverse, averse. 'He is not adverse to an occasional brandy' (*Observer*). The word wanted here was *averse*, which means reluctant or disinclined (think of *aversion*). *Adverse* means hostile and antagonistic (think of *adversary*).

aerate. Two syllables. Not *aereate*.

affect, effect. As a verb, *affect* means to influence ('Smoking may affect your health') or to adopt a pose or manner ('He affected ignorance'). *Effect* as a verb means to accomplish ('The prisoners effected an escape'). As a noun, the word needed is almost always *effect* (as in 'personal effects' or 'the damaging effects of war'). *Affect* as a noun has a narrow psychological meaning to do with emotional states (by way of which it is related to *affection*).

It is worth noting that *affect* as a verb is usually bland and often almost meaningless. In 'The winter weather affected profits in the building division' (*The Times*) and 'The noise of the crowds affected his play' (*Daily Telegraph*), it is by no means clear whether the noise and weather helped or hindered or delayed or aggravated the profits and play. A more precise word can almost always be found.

affinity denotes a mutual relationship. Therefore, strictly speaking, one should not speak of someone or something having an affinity for another, but rather should speak of an affinity with or between. When mutuality is not intended, sympathy would be a better word. But it should also be noted that a number of authorities and many dictionaries no longer insist on this distinction.

agenda. Although a plural in Latin, *agenda* in English is singular. Its English plural is *agendas* (but see DATA).

aggravate in the sense of 'exasperate' has been with us at least since the early seventeenth century and has been opposed by grammarians for about as long. Strictly, *aggravate* means to make a bad situation worse. If you walk on a broken leg, you may aggravate the injury. People can never be aggravated, only circumstances. Fowler, who calls objections to the looser usage a fetish, is no doubt right when he says the purists are fighting a battle that was long ago lost. But equally there is no real reason to use *aggravate* when 'annoy' will do.

aggression, aggressiveness. 'Aggression in US pays off for Tilling Group' (*Times* headline). Aggression always denotes hostility, which was not intended here. The writer of the headline meant to suggest only that the company had taken a determined and enterprising approach to the American market. The word he wanted was aggressiveness, which can denote either hostility or merely boldness and assertiveness.

aggressiveness. See AGGRESSION, AGGRESSIVENESS.

aid and abet. A tautological gift from the legal profession. The two words together tell us nothing that either doesn't already say on its own. The only distinction is that *abet* is normally reserved for contexts involving criminal intent. Thus it would be unwise to speak of, say, a benefactor abetting the construction of a church or youth club. Other redundant expressions dear to lawyers are 'null and void', 'ways and means' and 'without let or hindrance'.

alias, alibi. Both words derive from the Latin root *alius* (meaning 'other'). *Alias* refers to an assumed name and pertains only to names. It would be incorrect to speak of an impostor passing himself off under the alias of being a doctor.

Alibi is a much more contentious word. In legal parlance it refers to a plea by an accused person that he was elsewhere at the time he was alleged to have committed a crime. More commonly it is used to mean any excuse. Fowler calls this latter usage mischievous and pretentious, and most authorities agree with him. But Bernstein, while conceding that the usage is a casualism, contends that there is no other word that can quite convey the meaning of an excuse intended to transfer responsibility. Time will no doubt vindicate him – many distinguished writers have already used *alibi* in its more general, less fastidious sense – but for the moment all that can be said is that in the sense of a general excuse, many authorities consider *alibi* unacceptable.

alibi. See ALIAS, ALIBI.

allay, alleviate, assuage, relieve. *Alleviate* should suggest giving temporary relief without removing the underlying cause of a problem. It is close in meaning to 'ease', a fact obviously unknown to the writer of this sentence: 'It will ease the transit squeeze, but will not alleviate it' (*Chicago Tribune*). *Allay* and *assuage* both mean to put to rest or to pacify and are most often applied to fears. *Relieve* is the more general term and covers all these meanings.

allegory. See FABLE, PARABLE, ALLEGORY, MYTH.

alleviate. See ALLAY, ALLEVIATE, ASSUAGE, RELIEVE.

all right. A good case could be made for shortening *all right* to *alright*. Not only do most of us pronounce it as one word, but also there are very good precedents in *already*, *almost* and *altogether*, which were formed by contracting *all ready*, *all most* and *all together*, and even in *alone*, which was originally *all one*. In fact, many writers

– all too many, as it happens – appear to think that *alright* has gained acceptance already, as these two examples show: 'You came away thinking: "The guy's alright"' (*Observer*); 'The engine cuts out and someone says: "Poor chap, I hope he will be alright"' (*The Times*). English, however, is a fickle tongue, and *alright* continues to be looked on as illiterate and unacceptable and consequently it ought never to appear in serious writing.

allusion. 'When the speaker happened to name Mr Gladstone, the allusion was received with loud cheers' (cited by Fowler). The word is not, as many suppose, a more impressive synonym for reference. When you allude to something, you do not specifically mention it. Thus it would be correct to write: 'In an allusion to the President, he said: "Some people make better actors than politicians"'. But you leave it to the reader or listener to make his own deduction about what it is specifically you are implying. The word therefore is closer in meaning to implication or suggestion.

along with. See TOGETHER WITH, ALONG WITH.

altercation. 'Three youths were slightly injured in the altercation' (*Chicago Tribune*). No one ever gets physically hurt in an altercation. It is a heated exchange of words and nothing more.

alternative. Although the word derives from the Latin *alter*, meaning 'either of two', almost all the authorities agree that a strict interpretation of its meaning is needlessly pedantic and impractical. Only Partridge insists that three alternatives would be wrong.

Alternative and *alternate* are frequently confused, particularly in their adverbial forms. *Alternate* means by turns: first one, then the other. Day alternates with night. *Alternative* means offering a choice. The most common misuse is seen here: 'The journey may be made by road or alternately by rail' (cited by Fowler). The writer meant *alternatively* – though in fact the sentence would say no less without it. *Alternative* is in any case better avoided when there is no suggestion of a compulsion to choose. An army under attack has the alternative of fighting or retreating, but it is loose to say that someone has the alternative of making a journey by road or by rail when he might well choose not to go at all.

although. See THOUGH, ALTHOUGH.

ambiguous, equivocal. Both mean vague and open to more than one interpretation. But whereas an ambiguous statement may be vague by accident or by design, an equivocal one is calculatedly unclear.

ambivalent. 'It makes an ideal compromise for those who have always been ambivalent about Spain in high season' (*Guardian*). *Ambivalent* is better avoided when all you mean is of two minds or indecisive or ambiguous. Strictly speaking, it refers to a psychological state in which a person suffers from two irreconcilable desires. By extension, according to most authorities, it may be used to denote a situation involving strongly contradictory or conflicting views. But its use in any other sense is, as Partridge would say, catachrestic.

amid, among. 'Throughout the afternoon and evening the rescuers searched among the rubble for survivors' (*Guardian*). *Among* (or *amongst*) applies to things that can be separated and counted, *amid* (or *amidst*) to things that cannot. Since the rescuers were not searching one rubble and then another rubble, the word here should have been *amid*.

among. See AMID, AMONG; BETWEEN, AMONG.

amoral, immoral. Occasionally confused. Something that is immoral is evil or dissolute and contrary to the prevailing creed. The word amoral pertains to matters in which the question of morality is disregarded or does not arise. Thus an amoral person (one who does not distinguish between right and wrong) may commit an immoral act.

The use of the Greek prefix *a-* with the Latin-derived word *moral* pained Fowler, who suggested that *nonmoral* would be an improvement. But even he conceded that such a view was largely wistful. Today *nonmoral* is entirely acceptable, but only a pedagogue would insist on it.

an. See A, AN.

ancient. '[She] drew up in a car that can best be described as ancient' (*Observer*). Something that is ancient is not merely old, it is very old – at least several hundred years. A better word here would be *antiquated*, which refers to things that are out of fashion or no longer produced.

and. The belief that *and* should not be used to begin a sentence is without foundation. And that's all there is to it.

A thornier problem is seen here: 'The group has interests in Germany, Australia, Japan and intends to expand into North America next year' (*The Times*). This is what Fowler calls bastard enumeration and Bernstein, with more delicacy, calls a series out of control. The problem is that the closing clause ('intends to expand into North America next year') does not belong to the series that precedes it. It is a separate thought. The sentence should say: 'The group has interests in Germany, Australia *and* Japan, and intends to expand into North America next year'. (Note that the inclusion of a comma after 'Japan' helps to signal that the series has ended and a new clause is beginning.)

The same problem is seen here: 'Department of Trade officials, tax and accountancy experts were to be involved at an early stage in the investigation' (*Guardian*). *And* here is being asked to do two jobs at once: to mark the end of a series and to join 'tax' and 'accountancy' to 'experts'. It isn't up to it. The sentence needs to say: 'Department of Trade officials *and* tax and accountancy experts'. This reluctance by writers to supply a second *and* is common, but always misguided.

and/or. Bernstein calls this construction 'both a visual and a mental abomination' and he is right. If you mean *and* say 'and', if you mean *or* say 'or'. In the rare instance when you really do mean both, as in 'a $100 fine and/or 30 days in jail', say 'a $100 fine or 30 days in jail or both'.

and which. 'The rights issue, the largest so far this year and which was not unexpected, will be used to fund expansion plans' (*The Times*). *And which* should almost always be preceded by a parallel *which*. The sentence above would be unexceptionable, and would read more smoothly, if it were changed to: 'The rights issue, which was the largest so far this year and which was not unexpected . . .'. Occasionally the need for euphony may excuse the absence of the first *which*, but such instances are rare and usually the omission is no more than a sign of slipshod writing. The rule applies equally to such constructions as *and that, and who, but which* and *but who*. (See also THAT, WHICH).

another. 'Some 400 workers were laid off at the Liverpool factory and another 150 in Bristol' (*Daily Telegraph*). Strictly speaking, *another* should be used to equate two things of equal size and type. In this instance it would be correct only if 400 workers were being laid off in Bristol also. It would be better to write 'and 150 more [or others] in Bristol'.

anticipate. 'First-year losses in the video division were greater than anticipated' (*The Times*). To anticipate something is to look ahead to it and prepare for it, not to make a reasonable estimate, as was apparently intended here. A tennis player who anticipates his opponent's next shot doesn't just guess where it is going to go, he is there waiting for it. The word is only vaguely a synonym for expect. Grammarians, in a mercifully rare stab at humour, sometimes quote the old joke about an engaged couple who anticipated marriage – the point being that anticipating a marriage is quite a different matter from expecting one. In the example above, the use of the word is contradictory. If the company had anticipated the losses, it wouldn't have found them larger than expected.

anxious. Since *anxious* comes from *anxiety*, it should contain some connotation of being worried or fearful and not merely eager or expectant. You may be anxious to put some unpleasant task behind you, but, unless you have invested money in it, you are unlikely to be anxious to see a new play.

anybody, anyone, anything, any time, anyway, anywhere. *Any time* is always two words, *anything* and *anywhere* always one. The others are normally one word, except when the emphasis is on the second element (e.g., 'He received three job offers, but any one would have suited him').

A common fault occurs here: 'Anyone can relax, so long as they don't care whether they or anyone else ever actually gets anything done' (*Observer*). *Anyone* and *anybody* are singular and should be followed by singular pronouns and verbs. The sentence would be more grammatical as 'so long as he doesn't care whether he or anyone else ever actually gets anything done'. For a discussion, see NUMBER(4).

anyone. See ANYBODY, ANYONE, ANYTHING, ANY TIME ANYWAY, ANYWHERE.

anything. See ANYBODY, ANYONE, ANYTHING, ANY TIME, ANYWAY, ANYWHERE.

any time. See ANYBODY, ANYONE, ANYTHING, ANY TIME, ANYWAY, ANYWHERE.

anyway. See ANYBODY, ANYONE, ANYTHING, ANY TIME, ANYWAY, ANYWHERE.

anywhere. See ANYBODY, ANYONE, ANYTHING, ANY TIME, ANYWAY, ANYWHERE.

appendices, appendixes. Either is correct. *The Concise Oxford* prefers the first, *The American Heritage* prefers the second.

appendixes. See APPENDICES, APPENDIXES.

appraise, apprise. 'No decision was likely, he said, until they had been appraised of the damage' (*Sunday Times*). The word wanted here was *apprise*, which means to inform. *Appraise* means to assess or evaluate. An insurance assessor appraises damage and apprises owners.

appreciate has a slightly more specific meaning than many writers give it. If you appreciate something, you value it ('I appreciate your help') or you understand it sympathetically ('I appreciate your plight'). But when there is no sense of sympathy or gratitude or esteem (as in 'I appreciate what you're saying, but I think it's nonsense'), 'understand' or 'recognize' would be better.

apprise. See APPRAISE, APPRISE.

approximate means 'near to', so *very approximate* ought to mean 'very near to'. The difficulty is that when most people speak of a very approximate estimate, they mean a very tentative one, not a very close one. Gowers, in *The Complete Plain Words*, roundly criticizes the usage as loose and misleading. But Fowler classes it among his 'sturdy indefensibles' – words and phrases that are clearly illogical, and perhaps even lamentable, but which have become so firmly entrenched that the purists may as well throw in their towels. In this Fowler is no doubt right.

Where the authorities do find common ground is in the belief that *approximate* and *approximately* are cumbersome words and are usually better replaced by 'about' or 'almost' or 'nearly'.

a priori, prima facie. Occasionally confused. *Prima facie*, meaning 'at first sight' or 'on the surface of it', refers to matters in which not all of the evidence has been collected, but in which such evidence as there is points to certain conclusions. *A priori* refers to conclusions drawn from assumptions rather than experience.

apt. See LIABLE, LIKELY, APT, PRONE.

arbitrate, mediate. The functions of these two words are quite separate. Arbitrators are like judges in that they are appointed to hear evidence and then to make a decision. They remain aloof from the disputing parties. Mediators, on the other hand, are more like negotiators in that they shuttle between opposing sides trying to work out a compromise or settlement. They do not make judgements.

Difficulties sometimes also arise in distinguishing between an arbitrator and an arbiter. Whereas an arbitrator is appointed, an arbiter is someone whose opinions are valued but in whom there is no vested authority. Fowler sums up the distinction neatly: 'An arbiter acts arbitrarily; an arbitrator must not'.

argot. See JARGON, ARGOT, LINGUA FRANCA.

aroma does not refer to any smell, but only to pleasant ones. Thus 'the pungent aroma of a cattleyard' (*Washington Post*) is wrong.

arrogate. See ABDICATE, ABROGATE, ABJURE, ADJURE, ARRO-GATE, DEROGATE.

artefact, artifact. The first spelling is preferred in Britain, the second in America, but either is correct. In either case it is something shaped by human hand and not merely any very old object, as was apparently thought here: 'The team found bones and other artefacts at the site' (*Guardian*). Bones are not artefacts. The word is related to *artifice*, *artificial* and *artisan*, all of which imply the work of man.

articles, omitted. Some writers, in an apparent effort to make their writing punchier, adopt a habit of dropping the word *the* at the start of sentences, as in the three following examples, all from *The Times*: 'Monthly premium is £1.75'; 'Main feature of the property is an Olympic-sized swimming pool'; 'Dividend is again being passed'. Inevitable result is stilted sentences. Reader is apt to find it annoying. Writer who does it persistently should have his typewriter taken away.

artifact. See ARTEFACT, ARTIFACT.

as. See LIKE, AS.

as ... as. 'Housing conditions in Toxteth may be as bad, if not worse than, any in Britain' (*Observer*). The problem here is what grammarians call an incomplete alternative comparison. If we remove the 'if not worse' phrase from the sentence, the problem becomes clearer: 'Housing conditions in Toxteth may be as bad ... than any in Britain'. The writer has left the 'as bad' phrase dangling incompleted. The sentence should say 'as bad *as*, if not worse than, any in Britain'.

assassin. Until fairly recently the word applied not just to murderers, but also to those who attempted to murder, so to talk of a "would-be assassin' or 'a failed assassin' would be tautological. But, because of the proliferation of such crimes in the last twenty years, an assassin today is taken to mean someone who succeeds in his attempt. Thus there can no longer be any objection to appending a qualifying adjective to the word.

assuage. See ALLAY, ALLEVIATE, ASSUAGE, RELIEVE.

attain. 'The uncomfortable debt level attained at the end of the financial year has now been eased' (*The Times*). *Attain*, like 'achieve' and 'accomplish', suggests the reaching of a desired goal. Since an uncomfortable debt level is hardly desirable, it would have been better to change the word (to 'prevailing', for example) or, in this instance, to delete it.

auspicious. Beloved by public speakers ('On this auspicious occasion'), the word does not simply mean special or memorable. It means propitious, promising, of good omen.

avenge, revenge. Generally, *avenge* indicates the settling of a score or the redressing of an injustice. It is more dispassionate than *revenge*, which indicates retaliation taken largely for the sake of personal satisfaction. The corresponding nouns are *vengeance* and *revenge*.

average. 'The average wage in Australia is now about £150 a week, though many people earn much more' (*The Times*). And many earn much less. That is what makes £150 the average. When expressing an average figure, it is generally unnecessary, and frequently fatuous, to elaborate on it. (See also MEAN, MEDIAN, AVERAGE.)

averse. See ADVERSE, AVERSE.

awake. For a word that represents one of life's simplest and most predictable acts, *awake* has an abundance of forms: *awake, awoke, awaked, awaken, awakened.* Specifying the distinctions is, as Fowler notes, a difficult business, but in any case they present fewer problems than their diversity might lead us to expect. There are, however, two problems worth noting:

1. *Awoken*, though much used, is not standard. Thus this sentence from an Agatha Christie novel (cited by Partridge) is wrong: 'I was awoken by that rather flashy young woman.' Make it *awakened*.

2. As a past participle, *awaked* is preferable to *awoke*. Thus, 'He had awaked at midnight' and not 'He had awoke at midnight'. But if ever in doubt about the past tense, you will never be wrong if you use *awakened*.

awfully. See TERRIBLY, AWFULLY, HORRIBLY, ETC.

awhile. 'I will stay here for awhile' is incorrect because the notion of 'for' is implicit in *awhile*. Make it either 'I will stay here awhile' or 'I will stay here for a while'.

⊡ B ⊡

bait, bate. 'Robin's exploits were listened to with baited breath' (*Mail on Sunday*). Unless Robin's listeners were hoping to catch fish, their breath was *bated*. The word is a cousin of *abated*.

barbaric, barbarous. *Barbaric* emphasizes crudity and a lack of civilizing influence. A loincloth might be described as a barbaric costume. *Barbarous* stresses cruelty and harshness and usually contains at least a hint of moral condemnation, as in 'barbarous ignorance' or 'barbarous treatment'.

barbarous. see BARBARIC, BARBAROUS.

basically. The trouble with this word, basically, is that it is greatly overused and generally unnecessary, as here.

bate. See BAIT, BATE.

bathos. From the Greek *bathus*, meaning 'deep', *bathos* can be used to indicate the lowest point or nadir, or triteness and insincerity. But its usual use is in describing an abrupt descent from an elevated position to the commonplace. It is not, as is sometimes supposed, the opposite of pathos, which is to do with feelings of pity or sympathy.

be (with a participle). Often a wordy way of getting your point across, as here: 'He will be joining the board of directors in March' (*The Times*). Why not just say: 'He will join the board of directors in March'?

before, prior to. There is no difference between these two except that *prior to* is longer, clumsier and awash with pretension. If, to paraphrase Bernstein, you would use 'posterior to' instead of 'after', then by all means use *prior to* instead of *before*.

behalf. There is a useful distinction between *on behalf of* and *in behalf of*. The first means acting as a representative, as when a lawyer enters a plea on behalf of a client. It often denotes a formal relationship. *In behalf of* indicates a closer or more sympathetic relationship and means acting as a friend or defender.

'I spoke on your behalf' means that I represented you when you were absent. 'I spoke in your behalf' means that I supported you or defended you.

behove (US behoove). An archaic word, but still sometimes a useful one. Two points need to be made:

1. The word means necessary or contingent, but is sometimes wrongly used for 'becomes', particularly with the adverb 'ill', as in, 'It ill behoves any man responsible for policy to think of how best to make political propaganda' (cited by Gowers).

2. It should be used only impassively and with the subject 'it'. 'The circumstances behove us to take action' is wrong. Make it, 'It behoves us in the circumstances to take action'.

bereft. 'Many children leave school altogether bereft of mathematical skills' (*The Times*, cited by Kingsley Amis in *The State of the Language*). To be bereft of something is not to lack it but to be dispossessed of it. A spinster is not bereft of a husband, but a widow is (the word is the past participle of *bereave*).

besides means 'also' or 'in addition to' and not 'alternatively'. Partridge cites this incorrect use: '... the wound must have been on the right side of his face – unless it was made by something besides the handle of the gear-lever'. Make it 'other than'.

between, among. There is a long-standing misconception, still tenaciously clung to by some, that *between* applies only to two and *among* to more than two, so that we should speak of dividing some money between the two of us, but among the four of us. That is correct as far as it goes, but it doesn't always go very far. It would be absurd, for instance, to say: 'We sat down among the three lakes' or 'We decided to build our house among the forest and the town and the mountain'.

More logically, *between* should be used to indicate reciprocal relationships and *among* collective ones. If, for example, we referred to trade talks among the Common Market countries, it would suggest collective discussions, whereas trade talks between them could indicate any two of them meeting separately. *Between* emphasizes the individual, *among* the group.

A second problem with *between* is seen here: 'The layoffs will affect between 200 to 400 workers' (*The Times*). Used in this sense, *between* denotes the extremes of a range, not the range itself. Thus you should say either 'between 200 and 400' or 'from 200 to 400'.

between you and I. John Simon calls this 'a grammatical error of unsurpassable grossness'. It is perhaps enough to say that it is very common and that it is always wrong. The rule is that the object of a preposition should always be in the accusative. More simply, we don't say 'between you and I' for the same reason that we don't say 'give that book to I' or 'as I was saying to she only yesterday'. A similar gaffe is seen here: 'He leaves behind 79 astronauts, many young enough to be the children of he and the others . . .' (*Daily Mail*). Make it 'of him'.

biannual, biennial, bimonthly, biweekly. Biannual means twice a year and biennial means every two years (or lasting for two years). About that there is no trouble. Bimonthly (or bi-monthly) should mean every two months, but is often taken to mean twice a month. Similarly, biweekly (or bi-weekly) should mean every two weeks, but is often misconstrued as meaning twice a week. Clarity probably would be better served, at least with these last two, if you were to write 'twice a week', 'every two months' and so on.

biennial. See BIANNUAL, BIENNIAL, BIMONTHLY, BIWEEKLY.

bilateral. See UNILATERAL, BILATERAL, MULTILATERAL.

bimonthly. See BIANNUAL, BIENNIAL, BIMONTHLY, BIWEEKLY.

biweekly. See BIANNUAL, BIENNIAL, BIMONTHLY, BIWEEKLY.

blatant, flagrant. The words are not quite synonymous. Something that is blatant is glaringly obvious and contrived ('a blatant lie') or noisily obnoxious ('blatant electioneering') or both. Something that is flagrant is shocking and reprehensible ('a flagrant miscarriage of justice'). If I tell you that I regularly travel to the moon, that is a blatant lie, not a flagrant one. If you set fire to my house, that is a flagrant act, not a blatant one.

blazon. '[She] blazoned a trail in the fashion world which others were quick to follow' (*Sunday Times*). Trails are blazed. To blazon means to display or proclaim in an ostentatious manner.

blueprint as a metaphor for a design or plan is much overworked. If the temptation to use it is irresistible, at least remember that a blueprint is a completed plan, not a preliminary one.

born, borne. Both are past participles of the verb *bear*. *Born* is limited to the idea of giving birth ('He was born in December'). *Borne* should be used for the sense of supporting or putting up with ('He has borne the burden with dignity'), but is also used in the sense of giving birth in active constructions ('She has borne three children') and in passive constructions followed by 'by' ('The three children borne by her ...').

borne. See BORN, BORNE.

both. Three small problems to note:
1. *Both* should not be used to describe more than two things. Partridge cites a passage in which a woman is said to have 'a shrewd common sense ... both in speech, deed and dress'. Delete *both*.
2. Sometimes it appears superfluously: '... and they both went to the same school, Charterhouse' (*Observer*). Either delete *both* or make it '... they both went to Charterhouse'.
3. Sometimes it is misused for 'each'. To say that there is a supermarket on both sides of the street suggests that it is somehow straddling the roadway. Say either that there is a supermarket on each side of the street or that there are supermarkets on both sides. See also EACH.

both ... and. 'He was both deaf to argument and entreaty' (cited by Gowers). The rule involved here is that of correlative conjunctions, which states that *both* and *and* should link grammatically similar things. If *both* is followed immediately by a verb, *and* should also be followed immediately by a verb. If *both* immediately precedes a noun, then so should *and*. In the example above, however, *both* is followed by an adjective (deaf) and *and* by a noun (entreaty).

The sentence needs to be recast, either as 'He was deaf to both argument [noun] and entreaty [noun]' or as 'He was deaf both to argument [preposition and noun] and to entreaty [preposition and noun]'.

The rule holds true equally for other such pairs: 'not only ... but also', 'either ... or' and 'neither ... nor'.

bottleneck, as Gowers notes, is a useful, if sometimes overworked, metaphor to indicate a point of constriction. But it should not be forgotten that it is a metaphor and therefore capable of cracking when put under too much pressure. To speak, for instance, of 'a worldwide bottleneck' or 'a growing bottleneck' sounds a note of absurdity. Bottlenecks, even figurative ones, don't grow and they don't encompass the earth.

bravado should not be confused with bravery. It is a swaggering or boastful display of boldness, often adopted to disguise an underlying timidity. It is, in short, a false bravery and there is nothing courageous about it.

breach, breech. Frequently confused. *Breach* describes an infraction or a gap. It should always suggest *break*, a word to which it is related. Thus a breach of international law is a violation. *Breech* applies to the rear or lower portion of things. A breech delivery is one in which the baby is born feet first. A less common error is seen here: 'Washington remained hopeful that Secretary of State Cyrus Vance might breech the gap on his trip to the Middle East' (*Time*, cited by Simon). Here the writer was doubly wrong. He was apparently thinking of *breach* but meant bridge.

breech. See BREACH, BREECH.

bulk. A few authorities insist that bulk should be reserved for contexts involving volume and mass and not employed as a general synonym for 'the majority' or 'the greater part'. Thus they would object to 'the bulk of the book' or 'the bulk of the American people'. But two considerations militate against this view. First, as Fowler points out, *bulk* in its looser sense has been with us for at least 200 years and is unlikely now to slink off under the icy gaze of a handful of purists. And second, as Bernstein maintains, there is no other word that conveys quite the same idea of a generalized, unquantified assessment So use it as you will.

burgeon does not mean merely to expand or thrive. It means to bud or sprout and therefore indicates an incipient action. It would be correct to talk about the burgeoning talent of a precocious youth, but to write of 'the ever-burgeoning population of Cairo', as one writer on the *Daily Telegraph* did, is wrong. Cairo's population has been growing for centuries, and nothing, in any case, is ever-burgeoning.

but used negatively after a pronoun presents a problem that has confounded careful users for generations. Do you say, 'Everyone but him had arrived' or 'Everyone but he had arrived'? The authorities have never been able to agree.

Some regard *but* as a preposition and put the pronoun in the accusative – i.e., me, her, him or them. So just as we say, 'Between you and me' or 'Give it to her', we should say, 'Everyone but him had arrived'.

Others argue that *but* is a conjunction and that the pronoun should be nominative (I, she, he or they), rather as if the sentence were saying, 'Everyone had arrived, but he had not'.

The answer perhaps is to regard *but* sometimes as a conjunction and sometimes as a preposition. Two rough rules should help you:

1. If the pronoun appears at the end of the sentence, you can always use the accusative and be on firm ground. Thus, 'Everyone was there but him'; 'Nobody knew but her'.

2. When the pronoun appears earlier in the sentence, it is almost always better to put it in the nominative, as in 'No one but he knew'. The one exception is when the pronoun is influenced by a preceding preposition, but such constructions are relatively rare, often clumsy and usually better reworded. Two examples might be: 'To everyone but him life was a mystery' and 'Between no one but them was there any bitterness'. (see also THAN (3).)

But ... however. Since both words indicate a shift in direction, they should not appear together in a sentence. 'But that, however, is another story' should be 'But that is another story' or 'That, however, is another story'.

◉ C ◉

Caesarean. 'The baby, weighing more than 8 lb, was delivered by caesarian section' (*The Times*). The preferred spelling is *Caesarean* (upper-case 'C') in both Britain and the United States.

calligraphy. 'Both ransom notes have been forwarded to calligraphy experts in Rome' (*Daily Mail*). The writer meant 'graphology experts'. Calligraphy is an art. It means beautiful handwriting – so, incidentally, to talk of beautiful calligraphy would be redundant.

can, may. You have probably heard it a thousand times before, but it bears repeating that *can* applies to what is possible and *may* to what is permissible. You can drive your car the wrong way down a one-way street, but you may not (or must not or should not). In spite of the simplicity of the rule, errors abound. Here is William Safire writing in *The New York Times* on the pronunciation of *junta*: 'The worst mistake is to mix languages: You cannot say "joonta" and you cannot say "hunta".' But you can – and quite easily. What Safire meant was 'should not' or 'may not' or 'ought not'.

caption. Partridge objects to the use of *caption* to describe the words beneath an illustration, 'instead of above, as it should be', apparently on the assumption that the word derives from the Latin *caput* ('head'). In fact, it comes from *capere* ('to take'), and in any case the usage is now firmly established.

careen, career. Occasionally confused when describing runaway vehicles and the like. To careen in that sense should convey the idea of swaying or tilting dangerously. If all you mean is uncontrolled movement, use career.

career. See CAREEN, CAREER.

ceiling, floor. *Ceiling* used figuratively in the sense of an upper limit is a handy word, but, like many other handy words, is apt to be overused. When you do employ it figuratively, you should never forget that its literal meaning is always lurking in the background, ready to spring forward and make an embarrassment of your metaphor. Philip Howard cites the memorable case of the minister in the Attlee Government who excited confusion and exercised purists by announcing plans to put 'a ceiling price on carpets'. Better still perhaps was this two-faced headline in the *Daily Gulf Times*: 'Oil ministers want to stick to ceiling'.

Floor in the sense of a lower limit is, of course, equally likely to result in incongruities. Occasionally the two words get mixed together, as in this perplexing sentence, cited by both Howard and Fowler: 'The effect of this announcement is that the total figure of £410 million can be regarded as a floor as well as a ceiling'. (See also TARGET.)

celebrant, celebrator. 'All this is music to the ears of James Bond fan club members . . . and to other celebrants who descend on New Orleans each Nov. 11 . . .' (*The New York Times*). Celebrants take part in religious ceremonies. Those who gather for purposes of revelry are celebrators.

celebrator. See CELEBRANT, CELEBRATOR.

Celeste, Mary. The *Mary Celeste*, an American brigantine whose ten passengers and crew mysteriously disappeared during a crossing of the Atlantic in 1872, is sometimes used metaphorically – and almost always is misspelled, as here: 'At last, the sound of people in the City's Marie Celeste' (*Daily Mail*). Make it *Mary*.

celibacy. 'He claimed he had remained celibate throughout the four-year marriage' (*Daily Telegraph*). Celibacy does not, as is generally supposed, necessarily indicate abstinence from sexual relations. It means only to be unmarried, particularly if as a result of a religious vow. A married man cannot be celibate, but he may be chaste.

cement, concrete. The two are not synonyms. Cement is merely a constituent of concrete, which also contains sand, gravel, and crushed rock

centre round or **around** (US **center around**). 'Their argument centres around the Foreign Intelligence Surveillance Act' (*The Times*). *Centre* indicates a point, and a point cannot encircle anything. Make it 'centre on' or 'revolve around'.

chafe, chaff. The one may lead to the other, but their meanings are distinct. To chafe means to make sore or worn by rubbing (or, figuratively, to annoy or irritate). To chaff means to tease good-naturedly. A person who is excessively chaffed is likely to grow chafed.

chaff. See CHAFE, CHAFF.

chair (as a verb). 'The meeting, which is to be chaired by the German Chancellor, will open tomorrow' (*The Times*). A few authorities, among them Bernstein and *The New York Times Manual of Style and Usage*, continue to resist *chair* used in the sense of 'preside over', as it has been above. They would be happier if the quotation said something to the effect of 'The meeting, whose chairman will be the German Chancellor . . .'. Bernstein includes the usage among his 'fad words' – that is, words resorted to for no other purpose than effect. He rightly ridicules those writers who, in the pursuit of novelty, would 'elevator themselves to their penthouses, get dinner-jacketed and go theatering'. When *chair* first appeared as a verb (in the 1920s), it no doubt seemed just as ludicrous and contrived. But time has, I think, removed the sheen of presumptuousness from the usage, and most dictionaries, including the 1982 *Concise Oxford*, now accept it without comment.

choose. See OPT, CHOOSE.

chronic. See ACUTE, CHRONIC.

circumstances, in the and **under the.** Some newspapers, according to Partridge, insist on the first and forbid the second, which is unfortunate because they can be usefully distinguished. *In the circumstances* should indicate merely that a situation exists: 'In the circumstances, I began to feel worried'. *Under the circumstances* should denote a situation in which action is necessitated or, more rarely, inhibited: 'Under the circumstances, I had no choice but to leave'.

claim. Properly, *claim* means to demand recognition of a right. You claim something that you wish to call your own – an inheritance, a lost possession, a piece of land, for instance. But increasingly it is used in the sense of assert or contend, as here: 'There are those who claim that the Atlantic Treaty has an aggressive purpose' (cited by Gowers).

For years authorities have decried this looser usage and for years hardly anyone has heeded them. The battle, I think, is now nearly lost – even 69 per cent of the normally conservative members of *The American Heritage Dictionary* usage panel accept the word as a synonym for assert. But the authorities' case is worth hearing, if only because they remain so resolute in their dislike of the usage.

Their contention rests on the argument that there is no need for the word in its looser sense, and in this they are quite right. 'Assert', 'declare', 'maintain', 'contend', 'allege', 'profess' and even the much neglected 'say', 'says' or 'said' can almost always fit more accurately into the space usurped by *claim*.

But against this must be placed the weight of common usage, which is clearly imposing, and the fact (to quote Fowler, who doesn't like the word) that 'there is no doubt a vigour about *claim* – a pugnacity almost – that makes such words [as assert, etc.] seem tame by comparison'.

Whatever your position, it is worth bearing in mind that there are occasions when the word is clearly out of place. Fowler cites this headline from a newspaper in Hawaii: 'Oahu barmaid claims rape'. The suggestion appears to be that the unfortunate woman either contends she has committed a rape or would like one to call her own. Whichever, it is execrable.

climax. One or two authorities, notably Bernstein, continue to disapprove of *climax* in the sense of a culmination or high point. The word, they point out, comes from the Greek for ladder and properly ought to indicate a sequence in which each element is an advance upon the previous one. Fowler, however, raises no objection to its use as a synonym for culmination, and most dictionaries now give that as its primary meaning.

On two other points the authorities do agree – that the word should not be used as a verb ('The event climaxed a memorable week') and that it should never be used to indicate the lowest point in a series ('Our troubles reached their climax when the engine wouldn't start').

climb up, climb down. *Climb down*, as a few purists continue to point out, is a patent contradiction. But there you are. Idiom has embraced it, as it has many other patent absurdities, and there is no gainsaying it now. *Climb up*, on the other hand, is always redundant when *climb* is used transitively – which is to say most of the time. An exceptional intransitive use of *climb* would be: 'We sat down awhile before climb-ing up again'. But in a sentence such as 'He climbed up the ladder', the *up* does nothing but take up space. (See also PHRASAL VERBS and UP.)

close proximity is tautological. Make it 'near' or 'close to'.

co-equal. 'In almost every other regard the two are co-equal' (*Guardian*). A fatuous addition to the language. *Co-* adds nothing to *equal* that *equal* doesn't already say alone.

cognomen applies only to a person's surname, not to his full name or given names. Except jocularly, it is a pretentious and unnecessary word.

collectives. Deciding whether to treat nouns of multitude – words like *majority*, *flock*, *army*, *Government*, *group*, *crowd* – as singulars or plurals is entirely a matter of the sense you intend to convey. Although some authorities have tried to fix rules, such undertakings are almost inevitably, as Fowler says, wasted effort. On the whole, Americans lean to the singular and Britons to the plural, often in ways that would strike the other as absurd (compare the American 'The couple was married in 1978' with the British 'England are to play Hungary in their first World Cup match'). A common error is to flounder about between singular and plural, as here: 'The group, which *has* been ex-panding vigorously abroad, *are* more optimistic about the second half' (*The Times*). Even Samuel Johnson stumbled when he wrote that he knew of no nation 'that *has* preserved *their* words and phrases from mutability'. In both sentences, the italicized pairs of words should be either singular both times or plural both times.

collide, collision. 'The lorry had broken down when another car was in collision with it' (*Standard*). Such sentences, which are common in newspapers, are wrong in two ways. First, a collision can occur only when two or more *moving* objects come together. If a car runs into a wall, a lamp-post, a broken-down lorry or any other stationary object, it is not a collision. The second fault lies in the expression 'in collision with'. Many writers, anxious not to impute blame in articles dealing with accidents, resort to this awkward and inelegant phrase, but generally unnecessarily. From a legal standpoint it could be imprudent to say, 'Mr X's car collided with Mr Y's yesterday'. But rather than shelter under an ugly phrase, it would be just as safe, and much more idiomatic, to say: 'Mr X's car and Mr Y's collided yesterday'.

collision. See COLLIDE, COLLISION.

collusion. 'They have been working in collusion on the experiments for almost four years' (*Guardian*). *Collusion* should always carry a pejorative connotation, suggesting fraud or underhandedness. In the example above, describing the work of two scientists, the word wanted was cooperation or collaboration.

comic, comical. 'There was a comic side to the tragedy' (*The Times*). Something that is comic is intended to be funny. Something that is comical is funny whether or not that is the intention. Since tragedies are never intentionally amusing, the word wanted here was comical.

comical. See COMIC, COMICAL.

commence. 'The Princess' mother, who gave up modeling ... after commencing her not very happy marriage ...' (*Time*). An unnecessary genteelism. What's wrong with 'beginning'?

commiseration. See EMPATHY, SYMPATHY, COMPASSION, PITY, COMMISERATION.

common. See MUTUAL, COMMON.

comparatively. 'Comparatively little progress was made in the talks yesterday' (*Guardian*). Compared with what? *Comparatively*, like 'relatively' (which see), is better used only when a comparison is being expressed or clearly implied. It is better avoided when all you mean is 'fairly' or 'only a little'.

compare to, compare with. These two can be usefully distinguished. *Compare to* should be used to liken things, *compare with* to consider their similarities and differences. 'He compared London to New York' means that he felt London to be similar to New York. 'He compared London with New York' means that he assessed the two cities' relative merits. *Compare to* most often appears in figurative senses, as in 'Shall I compare thee to a summer's day?' So unless you are writing poetry or love letters, *compare with* is usually the expression you want. The distinction, it should perhaps be noted, is heeded more often in theory than in practice – *The American Heritage Dictionary* (Second College Edition), for instance, encourages the observance of the distinction in its entry for *compare* but then allows Henry Kucera to disregard the rule twice in his foreword – but it is a useful one and worth preserving.

A separate problem sometimes arises when writers try to compare incomparables. Fowler cites this example: 'Dryden's prose ... loses nothing of its value by being compared with his contemporaries'. The writer has inadvertently compared prose with people when he meant to compare prose with prose. It should be 'with that of his contemporaries'.

compassion. See EMPATHY, SYMPATHY, COMPASSION, PITY, COMMISERATION.

compel, impel. Both words imply the application of a force leading to some form of action, but they are not quite synonymous. *Compel* is the stronger of the two and, like its cousin *compulsion*, suggests action undertaken as a result of coercion or irresistible pressure: 'The man's bullying tactics compelled me to step forward'. *Impel* is closer in meaning to 'encourage' and means to urge forward: 'The audience's ovation impelled me to speak at greater length than I had intended'. If you are compelled to do something, you have no choice. If you are impelled, there is more likely to be an element of willingness.

compendium. No doubt because of the similarity in sound to 'comprehensive', the word is often taken to mean vast and all-embracing. In fact, a compendium is a succinct summary or abridgment. Size has nothing to do with it – it may be as large as *The Oxford English Dictionary* or as small as a scrap of paper. What is important is that it should provide a complete summary in a brief way. The plural can be either *compendia* or *compendiums. The OED* prefers the former, Fowler and most other dictionaries the latter.

complacent, complaisant. The first means self-satisfied, contented to the point of smugness. The second means affable and cheerfully obliging. If you are complacent, you are pleased with yourself; if you are complaisant, you wish to please others. Both words come from the Latin *complacere* ('to please'), but *complaisant* reached us by way of France, which accounts for the difference in spelling.

complaisant. See COMPLACENT, COMPLAISANT.

complete. Partridge includes *complete* in his list of false comparatives – that is, words that do not admit of comparison, such as 'ultimate' and 'eternal' (one thing cannot be 'more ultimate' or 'more eternal' than another). Technically, he is right, and you should take care not to modify *complete* needlessly. But there are occasions when it would be pedantic to carry the stricture too far. As the Morrises note, there can be no real objection to 'This is the most complete study to date of that period'. Use it, but use it judiciously.

compound. 'News of a crop failure in the northern part of the country will only compound the government's economic and political problems' (*The Times*). Several authorities have deplored the usage of *compound* in the sense of worsen, as it is employed above and increasingly elsewhere. They are right to point out that the usage springs from a misinterpretation of the word's original and more narrow meanings, though that in itself is insufficient cause to shirk it. Many other words have arrived at their present meanings through misinterpretation (see, for instance, INTERNECINE).

A more pertinent consideration is whether we need *compound* in its looser sense. The answer must be no. In the example above, the writer might have used instead 'multiply', 'aggravate', 'heighten', 'worsen', 'exacerbate', 'add to', 'intensify' or any of a dozen other words.

We should also remember that *compound* is already a busy word. Most dictionaries list up to nine quite distinct meanings for it as a verb, seven as a noun and nine as an adjective. In some of these, the word's meanings are narrow. In legal parlance, for instance, *compound* has the very specific meaning of to forgo prosecution in return for payment or some other consideration (it is from this that we get the widely misunderstood phrase 'to compound a felony', which has nothing to do with aggravation). To use *compound* in the sense of worsen in such a context is bound to be misleading.

Most dictionaries now recognize the newer meaning, so it would be imprudent to call the usage incorrect. But it is a usage we don't need and one that is better avoided.

comprise. 'Beneath Sequoia is the Bechtel Group, a holding company comprised of three main operating arms ...' (*The New York Times*). If you remember nothing else from this book, remember at least that 'comprised of' is always wrong. Comprise means to contain. The whole comprises the parts and not vice versa. In this example, the writer should have said 'a holding company comprising three main operating arms' or 'composed of three main operating arms'.

conceived. 'Last week, 25 years after it was first conceived ...' (*Time*). Delete 'first'. Something can be conceived only once. Similarly with 'initially conceived' and 'originally conceived'.

concept. People just cannot leave this word alone. Originally a concept was a general idea or theory derived from specific instances, and in that capacity it served us unassumingly for 400 years. Then, in the late 1960s, sociologists and politicians and advertising people discovered it. Suddenly the word was being equated with gracious living ('a new concept in urban lifestyles') or hard thinking ('conceptual framework') or diligent planning ('a media promotion concept'). Today, having squeezed the life from *concept*, they have gone looking for more pretentious variants and given us *conceptuate* and *conceptuant* and *conceptacle*. Very often the words hold no meaning at all, as in this advertisement from *The Age* cited by Kenneth Hudson: 'The personal characteristics of the appointee will include ... conceptual appreciation'. Such a phrase, as Hudson notes, is beyond comprehension. If all you mean is 'idea', use 'idea'.

concrete. See CEMENT, CONCRETE.

consensus. 'The general consensus in Washington ...' (*Chicago Tribune*). A tautology. Any consensus must be general. Equally to be avoided is 'consensus of opinion'. Finally, note that consensus is spelled with a middle 's', like 'consent'. It has nothing to do with 'census'.

consummate. As an adjective, the word is much too freely used. A consummate actor is not merely someone who is very good at acting, he is someone who is so good as to be unrivalled or nearly un-rivalled. It should be reserved to describe only the very best.

contact as a verb (as in 'I'll contact you next month') is still frowned on by most authorities, including almost two-thirds of the *American Heritage* usage panel. The authorities are right to object when a more specific word would do. But, as Bernstein asserts, there are times when the vagueness of *contact* can be useful. If I say, 'I'll contact you tomorrow', it leaves open the question of whether I will do it by phone or letter or telex, in person or through a third party. If English usage were in the hands of rational people like scientists and mathematicians, this expanded meaning would no doubt be considered a useful way of expressing a complex set of options simply. But English usage is not and the usage must be considered at best colloquial.

contagious, infectious. Diseases spread by contact are contagious. Those spread by air or water are infectious. Used figuratively ('contagious laughter', 'infectious enthusiasm'), either is all right.

contemptible, contemptuous. *Contemptible* means deserving contempt; *contemptuous* means to bestow it. *Contemptuous* gained currency in the sixteenth century – but too late to catch Shakespeare. In *Much Ado About Nothing*, he has Pedro declare that Benedick 'hath a con-temptible spirit'. He meant, at least by modern standards, contemptu-ous.

contemptuous. See CONTEMPTIBLE, CONTEMPTUOUS.

continual, continuous. *Continual* refers to things that happen repeatedly but not constantly. *Continuous* indicates an unbroken sequence. 'It rained continuously for three days' means it never stopped raining. 'It rained continually for three days' means there were some interrup-tions.

continuous. See CONTINUAL, CONTINUOUS.

contrary, converse, opposite, reverse. All four are sometimes confused, which is perhaps understandable since their distinctions tend to blur. Briefly, a *contrary* is a statement that contradicts a proposition. A *converse* reverses the elements of a proposition. An *opposite* is something that is diametrically opposed to a proposition. And the *reverse* can be any of these.

Take the simple statement 'I love you'. Its opposite is 'I hate you'. Its converse is 'You love me'. And its contrary would be anything that contradicted it: 'I do not love you', 'I have no feelings at all for you', 'I like you moderately'. The reverse could embrace all of these meanings.

conurbation. 'It was around dusk when the Union Jack replaced the Argentinian flag above the tiny conurbation of Goose Green' (*The Times*). A conurbation is a megalopolis where two or more sizable communities have sprawled together, such as Pasadena–Los Angeles–Long Beach in California or Bradford–Leeds in England. It can never be tiny.

converse. See CONTRARY, CONVERSE, OPPOSITE, REVERSE.

convince, persuade. There is a distinction worth preserving between these two words. Briefly, you convince someone that he should believe, but persuade him to act. It is possible to persuade a person to do something without convincing him of the necessity of doing it. *Persuade* may be followed by an infinitive, but *convince* may not. Thus the following sentence is wrong: 'The Soviet Union evidently is not able to convince Cairo to accept a rapid cease-fire' (*The New York Times*). Make it either 'persuade Cairo to accept' or 'convince Cairo that it should accept'.

country, nation. It is perhaps a little fussy to insist too strenuously on the distinction, but, strictly, *country* refers to the geographical characteristics of a place and *nation* to the political and social ones. Thus the United States is one of the richest nations, but largest countries.

crass means stupid and grossly ignorant to the point of insensitivity and not merely coarse or tasteless. A thing may be distasteful without necessarily being crass.

creole, pidgin. A pidgin – the word is thought to come from the Chinese pronunciation of the English 'business' – is a simplified and rudimentary language that springs up when two or more cultures come in contact. If that contact is prolonged and generations are born for whom the pidgin is their first tongue, the language usually will evolve into a more formalized creole (from the French for 'indigenous'). Most languages that are commonly referred to as pidgins are in fact creoles.

crescendo. 'David English, whose career seemed to be reaching a crescendo this month when he took over editorship of the stumbling Mail on Sunday ...' (*Sunday Times*). *Crescendo* is frequently misused, though only rarely trampled on in quite the way it has been here. It does not mean reaching a milestone, as was apparently intended in the quotation, or signify a loud or explosive noise, as it is more commonly misused. Properly, it should be used to describe a gradual increase in volume or intensity.

criteria, criterion. One criterion, two criteria. See also DATA.

criterion. See CRITERIA, CRITERION.

culminate. 'The company's financial troubles culminated in the resignation of the chairman last June' (*The Times*). *Culminate* does not mean simply the result or outcome. It indicates the arrival at a high point. A series of battles may culminate in a final victory, but financial troubles do not culminate in a chairman's resignation.

current, currently. It is a rare reader of newspapers these days who can venture all the way through an article without bumping into one or other of these – and very often a whole community of them. On one page of *The Times* in 1982 there were fourteen *current*s in residence, most of them conspicuously idle. At about the same time, *The New York Times* was providing sanctuary for six *current*s and a *currently* on one of its inside pages.

When there is a need to contrast the present with the past, *current* has its place. But all too often its inclusion is lazy and gratuitous, as in this example from one of the worst of the abusers, *Time* magazine: 'The Government currently owns 740 million acres, or 32·7% of the land in the U.S.'. Nothing would be lost if *currently* were deleted. Or take this sentence from the same article: 'Property in the area is currently fetching $125 to $225 per acre'. Why not save twelve characters and make it: 'Property in the area fetches [or, if necessary 'now fetches'] $125 to $225 per acre'?

currently. See CURRENT, CURRENTLY.

cut back. 'Losses in the metal stamping division have forced the group to cut back production' (*Daily Telegraph*). It would be more succinct to say 'have forced the group to cut production'. *Cutback* is often similarly pleonastic. 'Spending cutbacks' can almost always be shortened to 'spending cuts'. See PHRASAL VERBS.

dais. See LECTERN, PODIUM, DAIS, ROSTRUM.

dangling modifiers are one of the more complicated and disagreeable aspects of English usage, but at least they provide some compensation by being frequently amusing. Every authority has a stock of illustrative howlers. Fowler, for instance, gives us 'Handing me my whisky, his face broke into an awkward smile' (that rare thing, a face that can pass whisky), while Bernstein offers 'Although sixty-one years old when he wore the original suit, his waist was only thirty-five' and 'When dipped in melted butter or Hollandaise sauce, one truly deserves the food of the gods'.

Most often, dangling modifiers are caused by unattached present participles. But they can also involve past and perfect participles, appositive phrases, clauses, infinitives or simple adjectives.* Occasionally the element to be modified is missing altogether: 'As reconstructed by the police, Pfeffer at first denied any knowledge of the Byrd murder' (cited by Bernstein). It was not, of course, Pfeffer that was reconstructed by the police, but the facts or story or some other noun that is only implied.

Regardless of the part of speech at fault, there is in every dangling modifier a failure by the writer to say what he means because of a simple mispositioning of words. Consider this example: 'Slim, of medium height and with sharp features, Mr Smith's technical skills are combined with strong leadership qualities' (*The New York Times*). As written, the sentence is telling us that Mr Smith's technical skills are slim and of medium height. It needs to be recast as 'Slim, of medium height and with sharp features, he combines technical skills with strong leadership qualities' or words to that effect (but see NON SEQUITUR).

Or consider this sentence from *Time* magazine: 'In addition to being cheap and easily obtainable, Crotti claims that the bags have several advantages over other methods'. We can reasonably assume that it

---

* Strictly speaking, only adverbs modify; nouns and adjectives qualify. But because the usage problems are essentially the same for all the parts of speech, I have collected them under the heading by which they are most commonly, if not quite accurately, known.

is not Crotti that is cheap and easily obtainable, but the bags. Again, recasting is needed: 'In addition to being cheap and easily obtainable, the bags have several advantages over other methods, Crotti claims' (but see CLAIM).

William and Mary Morris offer a simple remedy to the problem of dangling modifiers – namely that after having written the modifying phrase or clause, you should make sure that the next word is the one to which the modifier pertains. That is sound enough advice, but, like so much else in English usage, it will take you only so far.

There are, to begin with, a number of participial phrases that have the effect of prepositions or conjunctions, and you may dangle them as you will without breaking any rules. They include *generally speaking*, *concerning*, *regarding*, *judging*, *owing to*, *failing*, *speaking of* and many others. There are also certain stock phrases and idiomatic constructions that flout the rule but are still acceptable, such as 'putting two and two together' and 'getting down to brass tacks'.

It is this multiplicity of exceptions that makes the subject so difficult. If I write, 'As the author of this book, let me say this', am I perpetrating a dangling modifier or simply resorting to idiom? It depends very much on which authority you consult.

It is perhaps also worth noting that opprobrium for the dangling modifier is not universal. The Evanses, after asserting that the problem has been common among good writers at least since Chaucer, call the rule banning its use 'pernicious' and add that 'no one who takes it as inviolable can write good English'. They maintain that the problem with sentences such as 'Handing me my whisky, his face broke into a broad grin' is not that the participle is dangling, but rather that it isn't. It sounds absurd only because 'his face' is so firmly attached to the participial phrase. But when a note of absurdity is not sounded, they say, the sentence should be allowed to pass.

They are certainly right to caution against becoming obsessed with dangling modifiers, but there is, I think, a clearer need than they allow to watch out for them. Certainly if you find yourself writing a phrase that permits the merest hint of incongruity, it is time to recast your sentence.

data. Many careful users of English continue to insist that we treat data as a plural. Thus 'Data from the 1980 census is unavailable' (*Los Angeles Times*) should read 'are unavailable'. To be sure, the purists have etymology on their side: in Latin, data is unquestionably a plural. The problem is that in English usage etymology doesn't always count for much. If it did, we would also have to write, 'My stamina aren't what they used to be', or, 'I've just paid two insurance premia'.

The fact is, of course, that for centuries we have been adapting Latin words to fit the needs and patterns of English. Museums, agendas, stadiums, premiums and many others are freely – and unexceptionably – inflected in ways that would have confounded Cicero. It may be time that we did the same for data.

There is a tendency these days to treat all Latin plurals as singulars, most notably criteria, media, phenomena, strata and data. With the first four of these the impulse is better resisted, partly as a concession to convention, but also because there is a clear and useful distinction to be made between the singular and plural forms. In stratified rock, for instance, each stratum is clearly delineated. In any list of criteria, each criterion (which is in fact of Greek origin but follows the same pattern) is distinguishable from every other. Media suggests – or ought to suggest – one medium and another medium and another. In each case the elements that make up the whole are invariably distinct and separable.

But with data such distinctions are much less evident. This may be because, as Prof. Randolph Quirk suggests, there is a natural tendency to regard data as an aggregate – that is, as a word in which we perceive the whole more immediately than the parts. Just as we see a bowlful of sugar as a distinct entity rather than as a collection of granules (which is why we don't say, 'Sugar are sweet'), so we tend to see data as a complete whole rather than as one datum and another datum and another. In this regard it is roughly synonymous with 'news' (which, incidentally, was treated by some nineteenth-century purists as a plural) and 'information'.

There is probably no other usage in English that more neatly divides the authorities. About half accept the word as a singular, though some only grudgingly. And about half are opposed to it, a few of them implacably. Fowler merely notes the existence of the singular usage but passes no judgement on it.

The shift is clearly in the direction of treating data as a singular, and a generation from now anyone who says, 'The data are here', may seem as fussy as the nineteenth-century newspaper editor* who sent one of his reporters a telegram asking, 'Are there any news?'

* The inquiry has been variously attributed to John Thaddeus Delane of *The Times* and to Horace Greeley of the *New York Tribune*.

(to which reportedly came the reply: 'No, not a single damn new'). But for now you are as likely to be castigated for your ignorance as you are to be applauded for your far-sighted liberalism. I vote for the singular, but until a consensus emerges, you are probably better advised to keep data plural, at least in formal writing.

decimate. Literally, the word means to reduce by a tenth (from the ancient practice of punishing the mutinous or cowardly by killing every tenth man). By extension it may be used to describe the inflicting of heavy damage, but it should never be used to denote annihilation, as in this memorably excruciating sentence cited by Fowler: 'Dick, hotly pursued by the scalp-hunter, turned in his saddle, fired, and literally decimated his opponent'. Equally to be avoided are contexts in which the word's use is clearly inconsistent with its literal meaning, as in 'Frost decimated up to 80 per cent of the crops'.

deduce, deduct. Occasionally confused. *Deduce* means to make a conclusion on the basis of evidence. *Deduct* means to subtract.

deduct. See DEDUCE, DEDUCT.

defective, deficient. To distinguish these two, it is necessary only to think of their noun forms: *defect* and *deficit*. When something is not working properly, it is defective; when it is missing a necessary part, it is deficient. *Defective* applies to quality, *deficient* to quantity.

deficient. See DEFECTIVE, DEFICIENT.

definite, definitive. *Definite* means precise and unmistakable. *Definitive* means final and conclusive. A definite offer is a clear one; a definitive offer is one that permits of no haggling.

definitive. See DEFINITE, DEFINITIVE.

demean. Some authorities, among them Fowler, object to the word in the sense of to debase or degrade, pointing out that its original meaning had to do with conduct and behaviour (by way of which it is related to *demeanour*). But, as Bernstein notes, the looser usage has been with us since 1601, which suggests that it may be just a bit late to try to hold the line now.

demise. 'The group has also been badly hit by the demise of the British shipbuilding industry' (*The Times*). *Demise* does not mean decline, as was intended here and occasionally elsewhere. Originally, *demise* described the transfer of an estate or title, usually as a consequence of a sovereign's death. By extension it came to be a synonym for death itself, but as such it is generally an unnecessary euphemism.

deplete, reduce. Though their meanings are roughly the same, *deplete* has the additional connotation of injurious reduction. As the Evanses note, a garrison may be reduced by administrative order, but depleted by sickness.

deplore. You may deplore a thing, but not a person. Thus 'We may deplore him for his conceit' (cited by Partridge) should be 'We may deplore his conceit' or 'We may condemn him for his conceit'.

deprecate. '. . . but he deprecated the significance of his achievement' (*Los Angeles Times*). *Deprecate* does not mean to play down or disparage or show modesty, as is often intended. It means to disapprove of strongly or to protest against.

de rigueur. Often misspelled, as here: 'A few decades ago when dinner jackets were de rigeur . . .' (*Daily Telegraph*).

derisive, derisory. Something that is derisive conveys ridicule or contempt. Something that is derisory invites it. A derisory offer is likely to provoke a derisive response.

derisory. See DERISIVE, DERISORY.

derogate. See ABDICATE, ABROGATE, ABJURE, ADJURE, ARROGATE, DEROGATE.

despite, in spite of. There is no distinction between the two. A common construction is seen here: 'But despite the fall in sterling, Downing Street officials were at pains to play down any suggestion of crisis' (*Daily Telegraph*). Because *despite* and *in spite of* indicate a change in emphasis, a shifting of gears, by the writer, 'but' is generally superfluous with either. It is enough to say: 'Despite the fall in sterling, Downing Street officials . . .'.

destroy is an incomparable – almost. If a house is consumed by fire, it is enough to say that it was destroyed, not that it was 'totally destroyed' or 'completely destroyed'. But what if only part of it burns down? Is it wrong to say that it was partly destroyed? The answer, contradictory though it may be, must be no. There is no other way of putting it without resorting to more circuitous descriptions. That is perhaps absurd and inconsistent, but ever thus was English.

diagnosis, prognosis. To make a diagnosis is to identify and define a problem, usually a disease. A prognosis is a projection of the course and likely outcome of a problem. *Diagnosis* applies only to conditions, not to people. Thus 'Asbestos victims were not diagnosed in large numbers until the 1960s' (*Time*) is not quite right. It was the victims' conditions that were not diagnosed, not the victims themselves.

dialect, patois. There is no difference in meaning between the two. Both describe the form of language prevailing in a region, though patois obviously is better reserved for contexts involving French or its variants. 'He spoke in the patois of Yorkshire' is at best jocular. The plural of patois, incidentally, is also patois.

differ, diverge. 'There now seems some hope that these divergent views can be reconciled' (*Daily Telegraph*). Linguistically, that is unlikely. When two things diverge, they move further apart (just as when they converge they come together). It is not a word that should be applied freely to any difference of opinion, but only to those in which a rift is widening.

different. Often used unnecessarily. 'The phenomenally successful Rubik Cube, which has 43,252,003,274,489,856,000 different permutations but only one solution ...' (*Sunday Times*); 'He plays milkmaid to more than 50 different species of poisonous snake' (*Observer*); '[He] published at least five different books on grammar' (Simon, *Paradigms Lost*). Frequently, as in each of these examples, it can be excised without loss.

different from, to, than. There is a continuing belief among some writers and editors that *different* may be followed only by *from*. At least since 1906, when the Fowler brothers raised the issue in *The King's English*, many authorities have been pointing out that there is no real basis for this belief, but still it persists.

Different from is, to be sure, the usual form in most sentences and the only acceptable form in some, as when it precedes a noun or pronoun ('My car is different from his', 'Men are different from women'). But when different introduces a clause, there can be no valid objection to following it with a *to* (though this usage is chiefly British) or *than*, as in this sentence by John Maynard Keynes: 'How different things appear in Washington than in London'. You may, if you wish, change it to 'How different things appear in Washington from how they appear in London', but all it gives you is more words, not better grammar.

dilemma. 'Indeed this was the dilemma facing the Bank of England. How could it coax people to help Laker?' (*Sunday Times*). The use of *dilemma* to signify any difficulty or predicament, as here, weakens the word. Strictly speaking, *dilemma* applies only when someone is faced with two clear courses of action, both of them unsatisfactory. Fowler accepts its extension to contexts in which there are more than two alternatives, but the number of alternatives should be definite and the consequences of each should be unappealing.

disassemble, dissemble. 'It would almost have been cheaper to dissemble the factory and move it to Wales' (*Sunday Times*). No it wouldn't. Unlike 'dissociate' and 'disassociate', which mean the same thing, *dissemble* and *disassemble* have quite separate meanings. *Dissemble* means to conceal. If someone close to you dies, you may dissemble your grief with a smile. The word wanted in the example above was *disassemble*, which means to take apart.

disassociate, dissociate. The first is not incorrect, but the second has the virtue of brevity.

discomfit, discomfort. 'In this she is greatly assisted by her husband ... who enjoys spreading discomfiture in a good cause as much as she does' (*Observer*). The writer here, like many before him, apparently meant *discomfort*, which has nothing in common with *discomfiture* apart from a superficial resemblance. *Discomfit* means to overwhelm, rout, defeat utterly.

discomfort. See DISCOMFIT, DISCOMFORT.

discreet, discrete. The first means circumspect, careful, showing good judgement ('a discreet inquiry'). The second means unattached or un-related ('discrete particles').

discrete. See DISCREET, DISCRETE.

disinterested, uninterested. 'Gerulaitis, after appearing almost dis-interested in the first set, took a 5–1 lead in the second' (*The New York Times*). A participant in a tennis match might appear un-interested, but he could never be disinterested, which means neutral and impartial. A disinterested person is one who has no stake in the outcome of an event; an uninterested person is one who doesn't care.

disorientated. *Disoriented* is shorter and usually preferable.

disposal, disposition. If you are talking about getting rid of, use *disposal* ('the disposal of nuclear wastes'). If you mean arranging, use *disposition* ('the disposition of troops on the battlefield').

disposition. See DISPOSAL, DISPOSITION.

dissemble. See DISASSEMBLE, DISSEMBLE.

dissociate. See DISASSOCIATE, DISSOCIATE.

distrait, distraught. The first means abstracted in thought, absent-minded. The second means deeply agitated.

distraught. See DISTRAIT, DISTRAUGHT.

disturb, perturb. The first is better applied to physical agitation, the second to mental agitation.

diverge. See DIFFER, DIVERGE.

double negatives. Most people know that you shouldn't say, 'I haven't had no dinner', but some writers, probably more out of haste than ignorance, sometimes perpetrate sentences that are scarcely less jarring, as here: 'The rest are left to wander the flat lowlands of West Bengal without hardly a trace of food or shelter' (*The New York*

Times). Since 'hardly', like 'scarcely', has the grammatical effect of a negative, it requires no further negation. Make it 'with hardly'.

Some grammarians condemn all double negatives, but there is one kind – in which a negative in the main clause is paralleled in a subordinate construction – that we might view more tolerantly. Evans cites this sentence from Jane Austen: 'There was none too poor or remote not to feel an interest'. And Shakespeare wrote: 'Nor what he said, though it lacked form a little, was not like madness'. But such constructions must be considered exceptional. More often the intrusion of a second negative is merely a sign of fuzzy writing. At best it will force the reader to pause and perform some verbal arithmetic, adding negative to negative, as here: 'The plan is now thought unlikely not to go ahead' (*The Times*). At worst it may leave the reader darkly baffled, as here: 'Moreover ... our sense of linguistic tact will not urge us not to use words that may offend or irritate' (Quirk, *The Use of English*).

doubt if, that, whether. Idiom demands some selectivity in the choice of conjunction to introduce a clause after *doubt* and *doubtful*. The rule is simple: *doubt that* should be reserved for negative contexts ('There is no doubt that ...'; 'It was never doubtful that ...') and interrogative ones ('Do you doubt that ...?' 'Was it ever doubtful that ...?'). *Whether* or *if* should be used in all others ('I doubt if he will come'; 'It is doubtful whether the rain will stop').

doubtless, undoubtedly, indubitably. 'Tonight he faces what is doubtlessly the toughest and loneliest choice of his 13-year stewardship of the Palestine Liberation Organization' (*Washington Post*). Since *doubtless* can be an adverb as well as an adjective, there is no need to add *-ly* to it. *Undoubtedly*, however, would have been a better choice still because, as the Evanses note, it has a less concessive air. *Doubtless* usually suggests a tone of reluctance or resignation: 'You are doubtless right'. *Undoubtedly* carries more conviction: 'You are undoubtedly right'. *Indubitably* is a pretentious synonym for either.

due to. Most authorities continue to accept that *due* is an adjective only and must always modify a noun. Thus, 'He was absent due to illness' would be wrong. We could correct it either by saying, 'He was absent because of [or owing to] illness', or by recasting the sentence in such a way as to give *due* a noun to modify, e.g., 'His absence was due to illness'.

The rule is mystifyingly inconsistent – no one has ever really explained why 'owing to' used prepositionally is correct, while *due to* used prepositionally is not – but it should perhaps still be observed, at least in formal writing, if only to avoid a charge of ignorance.

◉ E ◉

each is not always an easy word – even, it seems, for some authorities. Here are William and Mary Morris writing in *The Harper Dictionary of Contemporary Usage*: 'Each of the variants indicated in boldface type count as an entry'. As the Morrises no doubt knew but failed to note, when *each* is the subject of a sentence the verb should be singular – in this case 'counts'.

A plural verb is correct only when the sentence has another subject and *each* is a mere adjunct. Thus this sentence is also wrong: 'The Wimbledon and United States Open men's tournaments each has [make it 'have'] a first round of 128 players ...' (*The New York Times*).

Deciding whether to use a singular or plural verb isn't so difficult. When *each* precedes the noun or pronoun to which it refers, the verb should be singular: 'Each of us was ...'. When it follows the noun or pronoun, the verb should be plural: 'They each were ...'.

Each not only influences the number of the verb, it also influences the number of later nouns and pronouns. Simply put, if *each* precedes the verb, subsequent nouns and pronouns should be plural; if each follows the verb, the nouns and pronouns should be singular. Thus it should be: 'They each are subject to sentences of five years', but, 'They are each subject to a sentence of five years' (Bernstein).

each and every is at best a trite way of providing emphasis, at worst redundant and often both, as here: 'Each and every one of the 12 songs on Marshall Crenshaw's debut album is breezy and refreshing' (*Washington Post*). Equally to be avoided is *each individual*, as in, 'Players do not have to face the perils of qualifying for each individual tournament' (*The New York Times*). In both cases *each* alone would have been sufficient.

each other, one another. A few arbiters of usage (Simon, for instance) continue to insist on *each other* for two things and *one another* for more than two. There is no harm in observing such a distinction, but also little to be gained from it, and, as Fowler notes, the practice has no basis in historical usage.

economic, economical. If what you mean is cheap, thrifty, not expensive, use *economical*. For every other meaning use *economic*. An economic rent is one that is not too cheap for the landlord. An economical rent is one that is not too expensive for the tenant.

economical. See ECONOMIC, ECONOMICAL.

effect. See AFFECT, EFFECT.

effete. 'Nor is it a concern only to the highly educated, or the effete Northeast, or to city folk' (Edwin Newman, *A Civil Tongue*). *Effete* does not mean affectedly intellectual or sophisticated, as was apparently intended here, or effeminate and weak, as it is sometimes used. It means exhausted and barren. An effete poet is not necessarily either intellectual or foppish, but rather someone whose creative impulses are spent.

e.g., i.e. The first is an abbreviation of *exempli gratia* and means 'for example', as in 'Some words are homonyms, e.g., blue and blew'. The second is the abbreviation for *id est* and means 'that is' or 'that is to say', as in 'He is pusillanimous, i.e., lacking in courage'.

egoism, egotism. The first pertains to the philosophical notion that a person can prove nothing beyond the existence of his own mind. It is the opposite of altruism and is better left to contexts involving metaphysics and ethics. If all you wish to suggest is inflated vanity or preoccupation with the self, use *egotism*.

egotism. See EGOISM, EGOTISM.

either. 'But in every case the facts either proved too elusive or the explanations too arcane to be satisfactory' (Julian and Zelda Boyd, *The State of the Language*). *Either* should be placed before 'the facts' or deleted; for a discussion, see BOTH ... AND. For a discussion of errors of number involving *either*, see NEITHER.

eke. 'After a series of fits and starts yesterday the stock market eked out a gain' (cited by Bernstein). *Eke* means to add to or supplement in a meagre way. It does not mean to squeeze out, as was intended in the example above. You eke out an original supply – either by adding to it or by consuming it frugally – but you do not eke out a result.

elemental, elementary. *Elemental* refers to things that are basic or primary: 'Physiology is an elemental part of a medical student's studies'. *Elementary* means simple or introductory: 'This phrase book provides an elementary guide to Spanish'.

elementary. See ELEMENTAL, ELEMENTARY.

elicit, extract, extort. These three are broadly synonymous, but are distinguished by the degree of force that they imply. *Elicit*, the mildest of the three, means to draw or coax out, and sometimes suggests craftiness: you can elicit information without the informant being aware that he has divulged it. It shouldn't be confused with *illicit* ('unlawful'). *Extract* suggests a stronger and more persistent effort, possibly involving threats or importuning. *Extort* is stronger still and suggests clear threats of violence or physical harm.

empathy, sympathy, compassion, pity, commiseration. *Empathy* denotes a very close understanding of the feelings or problems of another. It is often employed as no more than a pretentious variant of *sympathy* and on the whole is better left to the psychologists. *Compassion* suggests a deeply felt understanding of the problems of others. *Pity* is rather more condescending; it suggests understanding of a problem intellectually but not emotionally. *Commiseration* falls roughly between compassion and pity, suggesting less emotion than compassion but more emotion than *pity*. *Sympathy* can cover all of these.

end result. Inescapably redundant.

enormity. 'The impression of enormity produced by the building ...' (cited by Fowler). *Enormity* does not, as is often thought, indicate size, but refers to something that is wicked, monstrous and outrageous ('The enormity of Hitler's crimes will never be forgotten'). In the example above, the writer should have said 'enormousness' – or, better still, found a less ungainly synonym.

enquiry. See QUERY, INQUIRY, ENQUIRY.

enthuse. '[They] are unlikely to enthuse over the news that the casino licensing appeal is due to start a week tomorrow' (*Observer*). *Enthuse* is a back formation – that is, a word coined from an existing word on the erroneous assumption that the new word forms the root of the old word. At some time in the past, someone seeing the noun *enthusiasm* assumed, wrongly, that it was formed from a verb *enthuse*. There is nothing inherently wrong with back formations – 'scavenge', 'laze', 'grovel' and even 'pea' (back formed from 'pease') were all usefully added to the language as a consequence of ignorance. But many other back formations – among them 'commentate', 'sculpt' and 'emote' – have failed to win complete acceptance because they are thought to be unnecessary or ungainly or to have too strong an air of novelty. As such they are better avoided.

envisage, envision. Both words suggest the calling up of a mental image. *Envision* is slightly the loftier of the two. You might envision a better life for yourself, but if all you are thinking about is how the dining room will look when the walls have been repainted, *envisage* is the better word. If there is no mental image involved, neither word is correct. A rough rule is that if you find yourself following either word with 'that' you are using it incorrectly, as here: 'He envisaged that there would be no access to the school from the main road' (cited by Gowers).

envision. See ENVISAGE, ENVISION.

epidemic. Strictly speaking, only people can suffer an epidemic (the word means 'in or among people'). An outbreak of disease among animals is epizootic. It may also be worth noting that *epidemic* refers only to outbreaks. When a disease or other problem is of long standing, it is endemic.

epitome is sometimes used as if it meant ultimate or unparalleled. In fact, it means typifying. 'The epitome of bad writing' is not writing that is quintessentially bad; it is writing that is representative of bad writing.

equable, equitable. Most dictionaries define *equable* as meaning steady and unvarying, but it should also convey the sense of being remote from extremes. A consistently hot climate is not equable, no matter how unvarying the temperature. Similarly, someone whose outlook is invariably sunny cannot be described as having an equable temperament. *Equitable*, with which *equable* is occasionally confused, means fair and impartial. An equitable settlement is a just one.

equally as is illiterate. 'This is equally as good' should be 'This is equally good' or 'This is as good'.

equitable. See EQUABLE, EQUITABLE.

equivocal. See AMBIGUOUS, EQUIVOCAL.

escalate is a useful word to describe an upward movement that is happening in stages, as in 'escalating taxes' or 'escalating warfare'. But many writers use it needlessly when they mean no more than increasing or accelerating. One writer, apparently uncertain just what he meant, referred to 'the increasing and rapidly escalating militarization of outer space' (*Time*). Since an escalating militarization must also be increasing, the phrase is redundant.

estimated at about. 'The crowd was estimated at about 50,000' (*Los Angeles Times*). Because *estimated* contains the idea of an approximation, *about* is superfluous. Delete it.

et cetera (etc.). 'Thousands competed, thousands watched and thousands also served – volunteers all of them – who only pinned numbers, massaged muscles, supplied water, charted positions, screamed encouragement, etc'. (*Los Angeles Times*). In lexicography and other more technical types of writing, *etc.* has its place. But in newspapers and magazines its use tends to suggest that the writer either didn't know what else he meant or, as in the foregoing example, was too lazy to tell us. Almost always it is better avoided.

evangelical, evangelistic. *Evangelical* is better reserved for contexts strictly pertaining to the Christian gospel. If you need a word to describe militant zeal, use *evangelistic*, e.g., 'The evangelistic fervour of the Campaign for Nuclear Disarmament'.

evangelistic. See EVANGELICAL, EVANGELISTIC.

eventuate. 'Competition for economic interest, power and social esteem can eventuate in community formation only if ...' (*British Journal of Sociology*, cited by Hudson). A pompous synonym for 'result'.

ever. 'On Wall Street, a late rally provided shares with their largest ever one-day rise' (*The Times*). Some people object to *ever* in the sense used here on the grounds that it covers the future as well as the past, and we cannot possibly know what Wall Street shares, or anything else, will be doing tomorrow.

Such an interpretation is a trifle short-sighted for two reasons. First, it fails to acknowledge that the usage has been established in Britain for almost sixty years and in America for nearer eighty; even if we accepted the purists' reasoning, we could defend the usage on grounds of idiom. But there is a more important consideration: to suggest that *ever* must always include the future is – or ought to be – clearly absurd. As an adverb, *ever* can indicate a span of time only to the extent that the verb will allow it – and a simple past-tense verb cannot push *ever*'s sense beyond the present. If I say, 'Have you ever been to Paris?' obviously I do not mean, 'Have you ever been to Paris or will you be going there sometime before you die?'

There may be a case for using *ever* sparingly. But to ban it arbitrarily is fussy and unidiomatic and can easily lead to ambiguity.

everybody. See NUMBER (4).

everyone. See NUMBER (4).

exception proves the rule, the. As a moment's thought should tell us, it isn't possible for an exception to confirm a rule – but then that isn't the sense in which the expression was originally intended. *Prove* here is a 'fossil' – that is, a word or phrase that is now meaningless except within the confines of certain common sayings ('hem and haw', 'rank and file' and 'to and fro' are other fossils). Originally, *prove* meant test (it comes from the Latin *probo*, 'I test'), so the sentence above meant – and really still ought to mean – that the exception tests the rule. It is bad enough to perpetuate a cliché without perpetuating it inaccurately. The original meaning of *prove* is preserved a bit more clearly in two other expressions: 'proving ground' and 'the proof of the pudding is in the eating'.

exigent, exiguous. The first means urgent and pressing or exacting and demanding; the second means scanty and slender. But both have a number of synonyms. If, like me, you weren't sure of the distinction until a moment ago, think how your readers will feel when you put them in the same position.

exiguous. See EXIGENT, EXIGUOUS.

exorbitant. There is a perplexing impulse among many writers on both sides of the Atlantic to put an 'h' into the word, as here: 'This is on the argument that they are troubled by exhorbitant interest charges' (*The Times*). Inhexcusable.

expatriate. Occasionally misspelled, as here: 'Kirov and other Russian expatriots . . .' (*Daily Mail*). Not to be confused with compatriot.

expectorate, spit. The distinction between these two is not, it must be conceded, often a matter of great moment, but still it is worth noting that there is a distinction. To spit means to expel saliva; to expectorate is to dredge up and expel phlegm from the lungs. *Expectorate* therefore is not just an unnecessary euphemism for *spit*, it is usually an incorrect one.

extort. See ELICIT, EXTRACT, EXTORT.

extract. See ELICIT, EXTRACT, EXTORT.

⊙ **F** ⊙

fable, parable, allegory, myth. Fables and parables are both stories intended to have instructional value. They differ in that parables are always concerned with religious or ethical themes, while fables are usually concerned with more practical considerations (and usually have animals as the characters). An allegory is an extended metaphor – that is, a narrative in which the principal characters represent things that are not explicitly stated. Orwell's *Animal Farm* is an allegory. Myths originally were stories designed to explain some belief or phenomenon, usually through the exploits of superhuman beings. Today, of course, the word can signify any popular misconception or invented story.

facade. 'Above the pilasters, on the front facade, is a five-story-high keystone ...' (*Time*). Although most dictionaries allow that *facade* can apply to any side of a building, it normally indicates the front (or face), and thus gives 'front facade' a ring of redundancy.

facile is usually defined as easy, smooth, without much effort. But the word should contain at least a suggestion of derision. Facile writing isn't just easily read or written, it is also lacking in substance or import. Unless a pejorative meaning is intended, the use of *facile* is, to quote Fowler, 'ill-judged'.

factious, factitious, fractious. *Factious* applies to factions; it is something that promotes internal bickering or disharmony. *Factitious* applies to that which is artificial or a sham; applause for a despotic ruler may be factitious. *Fractious* is that which is unruly or disorderly, as in 'a fractious crowd'.

factitious. See FACTIOUS, FACTITIOUS, FRACTIOUS.

farther, further. Insofar as the two are distinguished, *farther* usually appears in contexts involving literal distance ('New York is farther from Sydney than from London') and *further* in contexts involving figurative distance ('I can take this plan no further') or the idea of moreover or additionally ('a further point'). But there is, as *The OED* notes, 'a large intermediate class of instances in which the choice between the two forms is arbitrary'.

faze, meaning to disturb or worry, is sometimes confused with 'phase', as here: 'Christmas doesn't phase me' (*New York Review of Books* headline).

feasible. 'We ourselves believe that this is the most feasible explanation of the tradition' (cited by Fowler). Feasible does not mean probable or plausible. It means capable of being done. Its principal value, as Fowler notes, is as a substitute for 'possible' where the use of 'possible' might lead to ambiguity.

feet, foot. 'First, take a 75-feet hole ...' (*Daily Mail*); 'Twelve Paraguyan Anaconda snakes, each two foot long ...' (*The Times*). It shouldn't need pointing out that both of those sentences border on the illiterate.

We do not have 75-feet holes for the same reason that we do not have teethbrushes or necksties or horses races. In English, when one noun qualifies another, the first is almost always singular. There are exceptions – 'systems analyst', 'singles bar' – but usually they appear only when the normal form would produce ambiguity. When a noun is not being made to function as an adjective (as in the *Times* quotation above), the plural is the usual form. Thus a wall that is six feet high is a six-foot-high wall (for a discussion of the punctuation distinction, see HYPHEN in the appendix).

fever, temperature. You often hear sentences like, 'John had a temperature yesterday', when in fact John has a temperature every day. What he had yesterday was a fever. The distinction is not widely observed, even by some medical authorities. Bernstein cites the instance of a Massachusetts hospital that issued an official bulletin saying: 'Everett has no temperature'. Fowler excuses the usage as a 'sturdy indefensible', but, even so, it is better avoided in careful writing.

fewer, less. 'In the first four months of the year Rome's tourists were 700,000 less than in the corresponding period last year' (*Guardian*). Probably no other pair of words causes more problems, and with less justification, than *less* and *fewer*. The generally cited rule is that *less* applies to quantity and *fewer* to number. A rougher but more helpful guide is to use *less* with singular nouns (less money, less sugar) and *fewer* with plural nouns (fewer houses, fewer doctors). Thus the quotation above could be made either 'Rome's tourists [plural noun] were 700,000 fewer' or 'the number [singular noun] of tourists was 700,000 less'.

A particularly common error is the construction 'no less than', as here: 'There are no less than six bidders for the group' (*The Times*). This construction is so common, in fact, that it might be regarded as now having the force of idiom. Philip Howard for one allows it when he writes in *Weasel Words*: 'The watch with hands is an analogue device in no less than three different ways'.

Another problem worth noting occurs in this sentence: 'Representatives have offered to produce the supplements on one fewer press than at present ...' (*The Times*). Idiom, according to Bernstein, doesn't allow 'one fewer press'. You must make it either 'one press fewer', which is more grammatical, or 'one less press', which is more idiomatic.

A final type of problem occurs in this sentence: '... but some people earn fewer than $750 a year' (*The Times*). The difficulty here is that $750 is being thought of as a total sum and not as 750 units of $1. Make it 'less than $750'. Similarly it would not be incorrect to write, 'He lives less than fifty miles from London' because fifty miles is being thought of as a total distance and not as fifty individual miles.

finalize. 'But Cardin is, I gather, about to finalize plans for his China breakthrough' (*The Times*). An ugly and unnecessary word. What's wrong with 'complete' or 'conclude' or 'finish'?

first, firstly. The question of whether to write *firstly ... secondly* or *first ... secondly* or *first ... second* constitutes one of the more bizarre and inane, but most hotly disputed, issues in the history of English usage. Most of the animus has focused on *firstly* (De Quincey called it 'a ridiculous and most pedantic neologism'), though what makes it so objectionable has never been entirely clear. Fowler, ever the cool head, should perhaps be allowed the final word on the matter: 'The preference for *first* over *firstly* in formal enumerations is one of the harmless pedantries in which those who like oddities because they are odd are free to indulge, provided that they abstain from censuring those who do not share the liking'.

first and foremost. Choose one.

firstly. See FIRST, FIRSTLY.

flagrant. See BLATANT, FLAGRANT.

flak. Often misspelled, as here: 'Japanese women take a lot of flack from foreigners for their alleged docility' (*Observer*). The word, for what it's worth, is a contraction of the German *Fliegerabwehrkanone* ('anti-aircraft gun'), which contains nineteen letters, not one of them a 'c'.

flammable, inflammable. It is an apparent inconsistency of English that 'incombustible' describes an object that won't burn, while *inflammable* describes an object that will. Because the meaning of *inflammable* is so often misapprehended, there is an increasing tendency to use the less ambiguous *flammable*. In other cases this might be considered a regrettable concession to ignorance. But it would be even more regrettable to insist on linguistic purity at the expense of human safety.

flank. 'A Special Report on Finland tomorrow looks at the only Western nation that has to live with the Soviet Union as its neighbour on two flanks' (*The Times*). Two points to note here: the first is that a thing can have only two flanks, so the usage above would be tautological if it weren't inaccurate; the second point is that flanks fall on either side of a body. If I am flanked by people, they are to my right and left. Finland is flanked by the Soviet Union and Sweden, and not by the Soviet Union alone, which is to the east and south.

flaunt, flout. The confusion over these two is so widespread that at least two American dictionaries have granted them legitimacy as synonyms. The misusage is illustrated in this statement by President Jimmy Carter: 'The Government of Iran must realize that it cannot flaunt, with impunity, the expressed will and law of the world community'. To flaunt means to display ostentatiously, to show off. To flout, the word the President wanted, means to treat with contempt, to smugly disregard. There is every reason for keeping these meanings distinct.

floor. See CEILING, FLOOR.

flotsam and jetsam. In the increasingly unlikely event that you have need to distinguish these two, jetsam is that part of a shipwreck that has been thrown overboard (think of *jettison*) and flotsam that which has floated off of its own accord. Wreckage found on the sea floor is – or at least once was – lagan. There was, of course, a time when the distinction was important: flotsam went to the crown and jetsam to the lord of the manor on whose land it was washed up.

flounder, founder. *Founder* means to sink, either literally (as with a ship) or figuratively (as with a project). *Flounder*, which is thought to be a portmanteau word formed from *founder* and *blunder*, means to flail helplessly. It too can be used literally (as with someone struggling in deep water) or figuratively (as with a nervous person making an extemporaneous speech).

flout. See FLAUNT, FLOUT.

following, used carelessly, all too often results in unintentional absurdities, as here: 'The plumber was arrested in Virginia on a fugitive warrant following a 39-count indictment . . .' (*The New York Times*). The plumber was following the indictment that was following him? I think not. Here we have a doctor who is darting from tree to tree in pursuit of a medical inquiry, apparently while invisible: 'A family doctor has vanished from his home and surgery following an inquiry into his medical qualifications' (*Daily Mail*). What ever happened to 'after'?

foot. See FEET, FOOT.

forbid, prohibit. The words have the same meaning, but the construction of sentences often dictates which should be used. *Forbid* may be followed only by *to* ('I forbid you to go'). *Prohibit* may not be followed by *to*, but only by *from* ('He was prohibited from going') or by an object noun ('The law prohibits the construction of houses without planning consent'). 'They are forbidden from uttering any public comments' (*The New York Times*) could be corrected by making it 'They are prohibited from uttering [or forbidden to utter] any public comments'.

forced. See FORCEFUL, FORCIBLE, FORCED.

forceful, forcible, forced. *Forcible* indicates the use of brute force ('forcible entry'). *Forceful* suggests a potential for force ('forceful argument', 'forceful personality'). *Forced* can be used for *forcible* (as in 'forced entry'), but more often is reserved for actions that are involuntary ('forced march') or occurring under strain ('forced laughter', 'forced landing').

forcible. See FORCEFUL, FORCIBLE, FORCED.

forego, forgo. Commonly confused, as here: 'West Germans are proving unwilling to forego what many regard as their right to two or three foreign holidays a year' (*Financial Times*). *Forego* means to go before, to precede. To do without is to *forgo*.

forever, for ever. In American usage, *forever* is always one word. In Britain, traditionally it has been two words (Fowler insists on it), but more and more dictionaries now give *forever* as their first choice. *The OED* makes a distinction between *for ever* (meaning for all time) and *forever* (meaning continually).

for ever. See FOREVER, FOR EVER.

forgather. 'Wherever people foregather, one hears two kinds of talk ...' (John Simon, *Paradigms Lost*). Although *foregather* is not incorrect, the more usual spelling is *forgather*. A separate question is whether *forgather* adds anything that *gather* alone wouldn't say, apart from a creak of antiquity.

forgo. See FOREGO, FORGO.

former, latter. *Former* should refer only to the first of two things and *latter* only to the second of two things. Thus this extract is incorrect: 'There will be delegates from each of the EEC countries, plus Japan, Singapore, South Korea and Taiwan. Representatives from the latter ...' (*The Times*). Both words, since they require the reader to hark back to a previous reference, should be used sparingly and only when what they refer to is immediately evident. Few things are more annoying to a reader than to be made to re-cover old ground.

fortuitous. Not to be confused with fortunate, as it was here: 'If Mr Perella's merger assignment was mostly chance, it nevertheless was fortuitous' (*The New York Times*). *Fortuitous* means accidental or by chance, so the sentence above is telling us that Mr Perella's assignment was not only mostly chance, it was nevertheless entirely chance. A fortuitous occurrence may or may not be a fortunate one.

founder. See FLOUNDER, FOUNDER.

fraction. 'The gold recovered so far may represent only a fraction of the total hoard' (*Sunday Times*). A few purists continue to maintain that *fraction* in the sense of a small part is loose: $\frac{99}{100}$ is also a fraction but hardly a negligible part. The looser usage, however, has been with us for at least 300 years (Shakespeare employs it in *Troilus and Cressida*) and is unlikely to be misunderstood in most contexts. Even so, it would be more precise to say 'a small part' or 'a tiny part'. (See also PERCENTAGE, PROPORTION.)

fractious. See FACTIOUS, FACTITIOUS, FRACTIOUS.

frisson. 'A slight frisson went through the nation yesterday' (*The Times*). There is no other kind of frisson than a slight one. The word means shiver or shudder.

fruition has nothing to do with fruit. It derives from the Latin *frui* ('to enjoy') and formerly meant enjoyment. The sense in which it is most often used today – to describe the ripening or realizing of plans or the attainment of an end – is based on a misconception that took hold in the nineteenth century and reached its fruition (if you will) in this one. Today, Fowler alone rejects the word in its modern sense. No dictionary condemns it and most authorities consider it a useful addition to the language.

fulsome is one of the most frequently misused words in English. The sense that is usually accorded it – of being copious or lavish or unstinting – is almost the opposite of the word's dictionary meaning. *Fulsome* is related to *foul* and means odious and overfull, offensively insincere. 'Fulsome praise', properly used, isn't a lavish tribute; it is unctuous and insincere toadying.

further. See FARTHER, FURTHER.

future. As an adjective, the word is often used unnecessarily: 'He refused to say what his future plans were' (*Daily Telegraph*); 'The parties are prepared to say little about how they see their future prospects' (*The Times*). In both sentences *future* adds nothing and should be deleted.

⊡ G ⊡

gambit is often misused in either of two ways. First, it sometimes appears as 'opening gambit', which is redundant. Second, it is often incorrectly employed to mean no more than ploy or opportunity or tactic. Properly, a gambit is an opening move that involves some strategic sacrifice or concession. All gambits are opening moves, but not all opening moves are gambits.

gendarmes. Some dictionaries (*Collins*, for example) define *gendarmes* as French policemen. In fact, gendarmes are soldiers employed in police duties, principally in the countryside. Policemen in French cities and towns are just that – policemen.

gender. 'A university grievance committee decided that she had been denied tenure because of her gender' (*The New York Times*). *Gender*, originally strictly a grammatical term, became in the nineteenth century a euphemism for the convenience of those who found 'sex' too disturbing a word to utter. As such, its use today is disdained by most authorities.

germane, relevant, material. *Germane* (often misspelled 'germaine') and *relevant* are synonymous. Both indicate a pertinence to the matter under discussion. *Material* has the additional connotation of being necessary. A material point is one without which an argument would be incomplete. A germane or relevant point will be worth noting but may not be essential to an argument.

gerunds are verbs made to function as nouns, as in 'I don't like *dancing*' and '*Cooking* is an art'. There are two problems with gerunds:
   1. Sometimes the gerund is unnecessarily set off by an article and preposition, as here: 'They said that *the* valuing *of* the paintings could take several weeks' (*Daily Telegraph*). Deleting the italicized words would make the sentence shorter and more forceful.
   2. Problems also occur when a possessive noun or pronoun (called a 'genitive') qualifies a gerund. A common type of construction is seen here: 'They objected to him coming'. Properly, it should be: 'They

objected to his coming'. Similarly, 'There is little hope of Smith gaining admittance to the club' should be 'There is little hope of Smith's gaining admittance ...'.

The possessive form is, in short, the preferred form, especially with proper nouns and personal pronouns. For Fowler (who treated the matter under the heading 'fused participle') the possessive was virtually the only form. He insisted, for instance, on 'We cannot deny the possibility of anything's happening' and 'This will result in many's having to go into lodgings'. Most other authorities regard this as a Fowler idiosyncrasy and none would insist on the possessive for words that do not normally have a possessive form.

gift (as a verb). 'She talked easily of her own successes – a six-figure income, two wonderful children and the ability to gift her mother with a mink coat ...' (*Los Angeles Times*). A useful facet of English is its ability to turn nouns into verbs – we can man a boat, pocket some money, mother a child, people the earth – but is this one really necessary? No. (See CHAIR.)

gild the lily. The passage from Shakespeare's *King John* is: 'To gild refined gold, to paint the lily .../Is wasteful and ridiculous excess'. Nobody has ever gilded a lily.

glean. Originally the word applied to the act of going over a field after a harvest to gather the pieces that had escaped the reaper. Enough of its original meaning lingers that it should still convey the idea of gathering thoroughly and arduously, which the following sentence clearly does not: 'We can glean an indication of his vast wealth from the fact that he owns houses in London, Switzerland and California, with new or newish Rolls-Royces gracing each' (*Observer*).

glutton. See GOURMET, GLUTTON, GOURMAND.

gourmand. See GOURMET, GLUTTON, GOURMAND.

gourmet, glutton, gourmand. A gourmet is someone who takes a great deal of interest in, and trouble over, his food. A glutton is someone who enjoys food to excess and is not notably discriminating about what he shoves in his mouth. A gourmand falls between the two: he may be no more than a slightly greedier gourmet or no less than a glutton with some pretence of taste. In all instances, though, *gourmand* should convey at least a suggestion of disdain.

graffiti. 'There was graffiti in glorious abundance' (*Daily Mail*). *Graffiti*, meaning drawings or messages scrawled on walls and monuments, is a plural. Thus it should be 'There were graffiti ...'. If all you mean is a single embellishment, the word is *graffito*.

grammatical error is sometimes objected to on the grounds that a word or phrase cannot be simultaneously grammatical and erroneous, but must be either one or the other. In fact, the primary meaning of *grammatical* is 'of or relating to grammar', which includes errors of grammar, and in any case the expression is well established.

greater. 'The cost for a 17-year-old living in the greater London area ...' (*The Times*). 'In greater London' or 'the London area' says the same thing as 'the greater London area', but says it more simply.

grievous, not *grievious*.

grisly, grizzly. Occasionally confused. The first means horrifying or gruesome. The second means grey, especially grey-haired, and is a cliché when applied to old men.

grizzly. See GRISLY, GRIZZLY.

growth. Often used contrarily by economists and those who write about them, as here: 'It now looks as if growth will remain stagnant until spring' (*Observer*); '... with the economy moving into a negative growth phase' (*The Times*). Economists on the whole have had about as much beneficial effect on our language as they have had on our economies. *Growth* indicates expansion. If a thing is shrinking or standing still, *growth* isn't the word to describe it.

guttural. Often misspelled *gutteral*. Note the middle 'u'.

◉ **H** ◉

habits. 'As was his usual habit ...' (*Sunday Express*); 'The customary habits of the people of the South Pacific ...' (*Daily Telegraph*). Habits are always customary and always usual. That is, of course, what makes them habitual.

hail. See HALE, HAIL.

hale, hail. *Hale* means robust and vigorous, or to drag or forcibly draw (as in 'haled into court'), in which sense it is related to *haul*. *Hail* describes a greeting, a salute or a downpour. The expressions are 'hale and hearty' and 'hail-fellow-well-met'.

hamlet. 'Police searched his house in the tiny hamlet of Oechtringen ...' (*Observer*). It is in the nature of hamlets to be tiny.

hangar. All too often misspelled. The place where aircraft are kept is a hangar, not a hanger.

hanged. 'It was disclosed that a young white official had been found hanged to death in his cell ...' (*The New York Times*). 'Hanged to death' is redundant. So too, for that matter, are 'starved to death' and 'strangled to death'. The writer was correct, however, in saying that the official had been found hanged and not hung. People are hanged; pictures and the like are hung.

harangue, tirade. Each is sometimes used when the other is intended. A tirade is always abusive and can be directed at one person or at several. A harangue, however, need not be vituperative, but may merely be prolonged and tedious. It does, however, require at least two listeners. One person cannot, properly speaking, harangue another.

hare-brained. Occasionally misspelled, as here: 'The 22-year-old police constable dreamed up a "hair-brained and dangerous scheme ..."' (*Standard*).

head over heels is not just a cliché; it is also, when you think about it, a faintly absurd one. Our heads are usually over our heels.

healthful. See HEALTHY, HEALTHFUL, SALUTARY.

healthy, healthful, salutary. It is sometimes maintained that *healthy* should apply only to those things that possess health and *healthful* to those that promote it. Thus we could have 'healthy children', but 'healthful exercise' and 'healthful food'. There is no harm in observing the distinction, but there is little to be gained from insisting on it. If we are to become resolute, it would be better to focus on *healthy* in the sense of big or vigorous, as in 'a healthy wage increase', which is both imprecise and overworked.

    Salutary has a wider meaning than either of the other words. It too means conducive to health, but can also apply to anything that is demonstrably beneficial ('a salutary lesson in etiquette'). Most often, however, it is used to describe actions or properties that have a remedial influence: 'The new drug has a salutary effect on arthritis'.

Hebrew, Yiddish. The two languages have nothing in common except that they are spoken primarily by Jewish people. Yiddish (from the German *jüdisch*, 'Jewish') is a modified German dialect and thus a part of the Indo-European family of languages. Hebrew is a Semitic tongue and therefore is more closely related to Arabic. Yiddish writers sometimes use the Hebrew alphabet, but the two languages are no more closely related than, say, English and Urdu.

historic, historical. 'The Landmarks Preservation Commission voted yesterday to create a historical district on a gilded stretch of Manhattan's East Side' (*The New York Times*). Something that makes history or is part of history, as in the example above, is historic. Something that is based on history or describes history is historical ('a historical novel'). A historic judicial ruling is one that makes history; a historical ruling is one based on precedent. There are, however, at least two exceptions to the rule – in accountancy ('historic costs') and, curiously, in grammar ('historic tenses'). (See also A, AN.)

historical. See HISTORIC, HISTORICAL.

hitherto. 'In 1962, the regime took the hitherto unthinkable step of appropriating land' (*Daily Telegraph*). *Hitherto* means 'until now'. The writer meant 'thitherto' ('until then'), but 'theretofore' would have been better and 'previously' better still.

hoard, horde. Sometimes confused. The first describes an accumulation (usually hidden) of valuables. The second originally described nomadic tribes, but now applies to any crowd, particularly to a thronging and disorganized one ('hordes of Christmas shoppers').

Hobson's choice is sometimes taken to mean a dilemma or difficult decision, but in fact it means no choice at all. It derives from a sixteenth-century Cambridge stable-keeper named Thomas Hobson, who hired out horses on a strict rotation. The customer was allowed to take the one nearest the stable door or none at all.

hoi polloi. Two problems here. The first is that *hoi polloi* means the masses, the common populace and not the elite as is sometimes thought. The second problem is that in Greek *hoi* means 'the', so to talk of 'the hoi polloi' is tantamount to saying 'the the masses'. The best answer to both problems is to avoid the expression altogether.

holocaust. A holocaust is not just any disaster, but one involving fiery destruction. (In Greek the word means 'burnt whole'.)

hopefully. 'To travel hopefully is a better thing than to arrive'. Fifty years ago that sentence by Robert Louis Stevenson would have suggested only one interpretation: that it is better to travel filled with hope than to actually reach your destination. Today, however, it could also be read as meaning: 'To travel is, I hope, better than arriving'.

This extended sense of *hopefully* has been condemned with some passion by many authorities, among them Philip Howard, who calls it 'ambiguous and obscure, as well as illiterate and ugly'. Many others, notably Bernstein and Gowers, accept it, though usually only grudgingly and often with provisos attached.

Most of those who object to *hopefully* in its looser sense do so on the argument that it is a misused modal auxiliary – that is to say, that it fails to modify the elements it should. Consider this sentence: 'Hopefully the sun will come out soon'. Taken literally, it is telling us that the sun, its manner hopeful, will soon emerge. Even if we accept the sentence as meaning 'I hope [or *we hope* or *it is hoped that*] the sun will come out soon', it is still considered grammatically amiss. Would you say, 'Thinkingly the sun will come out soon' if you thought it might, or 'Believably it will come out' if you believed as much, or 'Hopelessly ...' if you hoped it wouldn't?

The shortcoming of that argument is that those writers who scrupulously avoid *hopefully* do not hesitate to use at least a dozen other words – apparently, presumably, happily, sadly, mercifully, thankfully and many others – in precisely the same way. In *Paradigms Lost*, John Simon disdains the looser *hopefully*, yet elsewhere he writes: 'Marshall Sahlins, who professes anthropology at the University of Chicago, errs some 15 times in an admittedly long piece'. That 'admittedly' is as unattached as any *hopefully* ever was. But Simon and others of his view would argue that 'admittedly' there is an absolute or sentence modifier – a word that can modify a whole clause or sentence and not just a single element in it.

To accept the one while excluding the other is, I think, curious and illogical and more than a little reminiscent of those Victorian purists who insisted that 'laughable' should be 'laugh-at-able' and that virtue would be served by turning 'reliable' into 'relionable'. All that distinguishes 'admittedly' and 'mercifully' and the others from *hopefully* is that the members of the first group have a pedigree. Yet feelings on the matter continue to run high. One American commentator recently said that acceptance of the looser *hopefully* would mark 'the final descent into darkness for the English language'. That's silly.

There are, however, two more compelling reasons for regarding *hopefully* with suspicion. The first is that, as in the Stevenson quotation at the beginning of this entry, it opens a possibility of ambiguity. Gowers cites this sentence: 'Our team will start their innings hopefully immediately after tea'. It isn't possible to say with any certainty whether *hopefully* refers to the team's frame of mind or to the time it will start batting.

A second objection is to the lameness of *hopefully*. If a newspaper article says, 'Hopefully the miners' strike will end today', who exactly is doing the hoping? The writer? The miners? All right-thinking people? All too often the word is used as no more than an easy escape from having to claim responsibility for a sentiment and as such is to be deplored.

But the real issue with *hopefully* has more to do with fashion than with linguistic rectitude. As *The American Heritage Dictionary* observes, the looser usage of *hopefully* is 'grammatically justified by analogy to similar uses of "happily" and "mercifully". However, this usage is by now such a bugbear to traditionalists that it is best avoided on grounds of civility, if not logic'.

horde. See HOARD, HORDE.

horribly. See TERRIBLY, AWFULLY, HORRIBLY, ETC.

host. As a verb ('He hosted the conference'), the word is a casualism that is not much needed and even less liked and is better avoided.

I, me. In 1981 *The Times* ran a series of articles under the heading 'Christmas and me'. Me cringed. Such lapses are not as uncommon as we might hope them to be. Consider, for instance: 'It was a bizarre little scenario – the photographer and me ranged on one side, the petulant actor and his agent on the other' (*Sunday Times*). At least the next sentence didn't begin: 'Me turned to the actor and asked him ...'.

Probably the most common problem with *I* and *me*, and certainly the most widely disputed, is deciding whether to write 'It was I' or 'It was me'. The more liberal authorities are inclined to allow 'It was me' on the argument that it is more colloquial and less affected, while the prescriptivists lean towards 'It was I' on the indisputable grounds that it is more grammatical. A point generally overlooked by both sides is that 'It is I' and like constructions are usually a graceless and wordy way of expressing a thought. Instead of writing 'It was he who was nominated' or 'It is she whom I love', why not simply say, 'He was chosen' and 'I love her'?

Things become more troublesome still when a subordinate clause is influenced contradictorily by a personal pronoun and a relative pronoun, as here: 'It is not you who is [are?] angry'. 'Is' is grammatically correct, but again the sentence would be less stilted if recast as 'You are not the one who is angry' or 'You aren't angry'. (See also IT.)

idiosyncrasy. Not idiosyncracy.

i.e. See E.G., I.E.

if. Problems often arise in deciding whether *if* is introducing a subjunctive clause ('If I were ...') or an indicative one ('If I was ...'). Simply put, when *if* introduces a notion that is clearly untrue or hypothetical or improbable, the verb should be in the subjunctive: 'If I were king ...'; 'If he were in your shoes ...'. But when the *if* is introducing a thought that is true or could well be true, the mood should be indicative: 'If I was happy then, I don't remember it now'. One small hint may help: if the sentence contains a *would* or its variants, the mood of the sentence is subjunctive, as in 'If I were you, I wouldn't take the job'. (See also SUBJUNCTIVES.)

if and when. Almost always unnecessary. Choose one or the other.

ilk. 'And it was because Oskar could play the part of brother to Amon and his ilk ...' (*Sunday Times*). The authorities are virtually – and perhaps a little curiously – unanimous in condemning *ilk* in the sense of type or kind, as it is used above. A Scots word, it means 'same'. 'McFarlan of that ilk' means 'McFarlan of McFarlan'. But in condemning the word the authorities fail to acknowledge that there is very little need for the word in its stricter sense inside Britain and no need at all outside. If we are to allow the broader meaning, we should at least not employ it redundantly, as it was here: 'Politicians of all stripes and ilks ...' (William Safire in *The New York Times*).

immoral. See AMORAL, IMMORAL.

impel. See COMPEL, IMPEL.

imply, infer, insinuate. The first two are all too often confused. *Imply* means to suggest: 'He implied that I was a fool'. *Infer* means to deduce: 'We inferred that he wasn't coming'. A speaker implies, a listener infers. *Inference* and *implication* are also sometimes confused, as here: 'Asked if he meant that the Russians were bluffing, the Secretary said ... that that was "a fair implication" ' (cited by Bernstein). The Secretary meant 'a fair inference'.

   Insinuate is similar to *imply* in that it describes an action not explicitly stated. But unlike *imply*, which can be neutral, *insinuate* always has pejorative connotations.

important, importantly. 'But more importantly, his work was instrumental in eradicating cholera' (*Sunday Telegraph*). Some authorities condemn *importantly* here on the argument that the sentence involves an ellipsis of thought, as if it were saying, 'But [what is] more important...'. Others contend that *importantly* is being used as a sentence adverb, modifying the whole expression, in much the same way as 'happily' in 'Happily, it didn't rain'. Both points are grammatically defensible, so the choice of which to use must be entirely a matter of preference.

importantly. See IMPORTANT, IMPORTANTLY.

impracticable. See IMPRACTICAL, IMPRACTICABLE, UN-PRACTICAL.

impractical, impracticable, unpractical. If a thing could be done but isn't worth doing, it is impractical or unpractical (the words mean the same thing). If it can't be done at all, it's impracticable.

in, into, in to. *In* normally indicates a fixed position: 'He was in the house'. *Into* indicates movement towards a fixed position: 'He went into the house'. There are, however, many exceptions (e.g., 'He put it in his pocket'). *In to* (two words) is correct when *in* is an adverb: 'He turned himself in to the police'.

It is perhaps also worth noting that *in* is the first word in a number of expressions that usually do no more than consume space: in connection with, in terms of, in respect of, in the event that, in view of the fact that, in the course of, in order to and in excess of. In the following two examples the italicized words would be better replaced by the word or words in parentheses: 'Profits were *in excess of* (more than) £12 million' (*Guardian*); 'Rationalization measures *in respect of* (at) the timber merchanting division . . .' (*The Times*).

inchoate. Probably because of the similarity in spelling to *chaotic* and in pronunciation to *incoherent*, the word is sometimes used in the sense of disorderly or disorganized. In fact, it means incipient, un-developed, just starting. An inchoate enterprise is likely to be dis-organized, but the disorderliness is not what makes it inchoate.

incline. As a verb, *incline* indicates a conscious decision, as in 'He was inclined to go to Greece for the summer'. When there is no choice involved, *incline* is incorrect, as it was here: 'Roads are inclined to deteriorate during bad weather' (*Daily Telegraph*).

include indicates that what is to follow is only part of a greater whole. To use it when you are describing a totality is sloppy: 'The company's three main operating divisions, which include hotels, catering and package holidays . . .' (*Guardian*); 'The 630 job losses include 300 in Redcar and 330 in Port Talbot' (*The Times*).

inculcate means to persistently impress a habit upon or a belief into another person. You inculcate an idea, not a person. 'My father in-

culcated me with a belief in democracy' should be 'My father incul-
cated in me a belief in democracy'. A simple guide: If you cannot
substitute 'implant', then *inculcate* is not being used correctly.

indefinitely. 'The new structures should, by contrast, last almost indefinitely' (*Newsweek*). *Indefinitely* in the sense of 'for a very long
time' is better avoided. The word means only 'without prescribed
limits'. Thus, strictly speaking, the sentence above is telling us that
the structures may last for a million years or they may collapse after
ten minutes. 'Almost indefinitely', incidentally, is impossible.

indexes, indices. Both *The Concise Oxford* and *The American Heritage*
prefer *indexes*. *The Concise Oxford* suggests, however, that *indices*
is better for technical applications. *The American Heritage* takes no
stand on usage.

indices. See INDEXES, INDICES.

individual is acceptable when you are contrasting one person with
an organization or body of people ('How can one individual hope
to rectify the evils of society?'). But as a synonym for person ('Do
you see that individual standing over there?') it is otiose.

indubitably. See DOUBTLESS, UNDOUBTEDLY, INDUBITABLY.

infectious. See CONTAGIOUS, INFECTIOUS.

infer. See IMPLY, INFER, INSINUATE.

inflammable. See FLAMMABLE, INFLAMMABLE.

inflation has spawned a number of variants, all of which need to be
used with care if they are to be used at all. *Inflation* itself means that
the money supply and prices are rising. *Hyper-inflation* means that
they are rising rapidly (at an annual rate of at least 20 per cent).
Deflation means that they are falling and *reflation* that they are being
pushed up again after a period of deflation. *Disinflation*, the ugliest
and most frequently misused of the words, means that prices are rising,
but at a slower rate, and *stagflation* means that prices are rising while
output is stagnant. The last two in particular are better avoided. There

is a separate point worth noting: if the rate of inflation was 8 per cent last month and 6 per cent this month, it does not mean that prices are falling; it means they are rising at a slower rate.

ingenious, ingenuous. The first means clever, the second means frank, unsophisticated, naive. Problems also sometimes occur with the negative form *disingenuous*, which means crafty or not straight-forward.

ingenuous. See INGENIOUS, INGENUOUS.

innocent. 'She and four other inmates have pleaded innocent to the tax charges' (*Boston Globe*). Under the British and American judicial systems, people do not plead innocent. They plead guilty or not guilty.

input, output. Gowers writes of a man who, every time he saw *input* and *output*, wanted to upstand and outwalk. The spread of computers and their attendant argot is now inescapable, but the use of *input*, at least outside contexts involving the processing of data, is better resisted. *Output* has gained wider acceptance and can be used to describe industrial and economic production, but elsewhere is still better replaced.

inquiry. See QUERY, INQUIRY, ENQUIRY.

insidious, invidious. *Insidious* indicates the stealthy spread of something undesirable ('an insidious leak in the roof'). *Invidious* means offensive or inviting animosity ('an invidious remark').

insinuate. See IMPLY, INFER, INSINUATE.

in spite of. See DESPITE, IN SPITE OF.

intense, intensive. *Intense* should describe things that are heavy or extreme or occur to a high degree ('intense sunlight', 'intense down-pour'). *Intensive* implies a concentrated focus ('intensive care'). Although the two words often come to the same thing, they needn't. An intense bombardment, as Fowler points out, is a severe one. An intensive bombardment is one directed at a small area.

intensive

intensive. See INTENSE, INTENSIVE.

interface. To a scientist an interface is the meeting place of two regions, systems or processes. For the rest of us it should suggest no more than a misguided attempt by the writer to impress his readers. 'Our social services group provides an interface for the different specialists concerned with the subject' (cited by Howard) is merely pretentious.

internecine. For more than 200 years writers have been using *internecine* quite wrongly in the sense of a prolonged or costly internal conflict. For this small error we can thank Samuel Johnson, who was misled by the prefix *inter-* and defined the word as 'endeavouring mutual destruction'. In its proper sense the word does denote extermination, slaughter or a bloody quarrel, but contains no sense of being mutually destructive. It has, however, been misused for so long that it would be pedantic, and wildly optimistic, to try to enforce its original meaning. As Philip Howard notes: 'The English language cannot be regulated so as to avoid offending the susceptibilities of classical scholars'. He does suggest, however, that the word should be reserved for bloody and violent disputes and not mere squabblings.

interpretative. See INTERPRETIVE, INTERPRETATIVE.

interpretive, interpretative. Either is correct.

interval. '... the training period was still three years, an interval widely regarded in the industry as being unrealistically long'. (cited by Gowers). An interval is the period *between* two events.

into. See IN, INTO, IN TO.

in to. See IN, INTO, IN TO.

intrigue. Originally *intrigue* signified underhanded plotting and nothing else. The looser meaning of 'arousing' or 'fascinating' ('We found the lecture intriguing') is now established. It is, however, greatly overworked and almost always better replaced by a more telling word.

invariably does not mean frequently or usually, as was intended here: 'Supersede is yet another word that is invariably misspelled' (*Chicago Tribune*). *Invariable* and *invariably* mean fixed, constant, not subject to change. Night invariably follows day, but no word is invariably misspelled.

inveigh, inveigle. Occasionally confused. The first means to speak strongly against ('He inveighed against the rise in taxes'). The second means to entice or cajole ('They inveigled an invitation to the party').

inveigle. See INVEIGH, INVEIGLE.

invidious. See INSIDIOUS, INVIDIOUS.

irony, sarcasm. *Irony* is the use of words to convey a contradiction between the literal and intended meanings. *Sarcasm* is very like irony except that it is more stinging. Where the primary intent behind irony is to amuse, with sarcasm it is to wound.

irregardless. *The Oxford English Dictionary* contains 414,825 words. *Irregardless* is not one of them. (There is, however, a perfectly good word 'irrespective'.) Make it *regardless*.

it. Sentences that begin with *it* are always worth a second look. Oftentimes an anticipatory or 'dummy' *it* is unobjectionable or even unavoidable ('It seems to me', 'It began to rain', 'It is widely believed that'), but perhaps just as often it is no more than a sign of circuitous and tedious writing. The two following examples came from one article in *The New York Times*: 'It was Mr Bechtel who was the more peripatetic of the two'; 'It was under his direction that the annual reports began'. Both sentences would be shorter and more forceful if 'It was' and the relative pronouns (respectively 'who' and 'that') were removed, making them 'Mr Bechtel was the more peripatetic of the two' and 'Under his direction the annual reports began'.

its, it's. The distinction between these two ought not to trouble a ten-year-old, but one article in the *Washington Post* in 1981 managed to confuse them five times: 'Its the worst its been in the last five years'; 'Its awful'; 'Its come full circle'; 'Its nice to see the enemy'.

It's

Its is the possessive form of *it*: 'Put each book in its place'. *It's*, which was intended in each of the examples above, is the contraction of *it is*.

it's. See ITS, IT'S.

⊡ J ⊡

jargon, argot, lingua franca. At a conference of sociologists in America in 1977, love was defined as 'the cognitive-affective state characterized by intrusive and obsessive fantasizing concerning reciprocity of amorant feelings by the object of the amorance'. That is jargon – the practice of never calling a spade a spade when you might instead call it a manual earth-restructuring implement. So long as it circulates only among a given profession, jargon is usually unobjectionable and frequently useful, since every profession needs its own form of shorthand. But all too often it escapes into the wider world, so that we have schools in Dallas sending parents a manual called 'Terminal Behaviour Objectives for Continuous Progression Modules in Early Childhood Education' (cited by Newman) and a critic who describes an artist as having 'the courage to monumentalize the polymorphous-perverse world of his inner quickenings' in a painting that contains 'the tall duration of a muralizing necessity that strains to leap its pendulum's arc while carrying a full weight on iconographic potency' (cited by Bernstein). This vacuous pretentiousness, this curious urge to speak of 'attitudinal concepts' when we mean attitudes and 'optimally consonant patterns of learning constructs' when we mean a sound education, is probably the greatest linguistic sin of the century.

Argot was originally the language of thieves, but has, like *jargon*, come to mean a way of communicating peculiar to a particular group. *Lingua franca* (literally 'the Frankish tongue') is any language or mixture of languages that serves as a common means of communication among diverse parties. English, for instance, is the lingua franca of international air travel.

join together, link together. The Bible and marriage ceremonies notwithstanding, *join together* is almost always tautological. Similarly *linked together*, even when written by as eminent a man as C. T. Onions: 'The first members of a group linked together by one of the above conjunctions ...' (in *Modern English Syntax*).

Jonson, Ben. The English dramatist and poet (1573–1637) has probably the most frequently misspelled surname in the literary world.

Even Bernstein calls him Ben Johnson (in *Dos, Don'ts and Maybes of English Usage*).

just deserts. Not *just desserts*. The expression has nothing to do with the sweet course after dinner. It comes from the French for 'deserve', which may help you to remember that it has just one middle 's'.

◦ K ◦

key. After 'major' (which see), *key* is perhaps the lazy writer's best friend. It can be appended to a multiplicity of nouns ('key decisions', 'key elections', 'key proposals') and made to cover a range of meanings from notable to essential. It spares the writer the annoyance of having to think of a more precise word and the challenge of making his writing interesting.

Khrushchev, Nikita. 'The man who adored Khruschev' (*Daily Telegraph* headline). Khrushchev may have been adored by one man, but he has been misspelled by many. Note that the name has three 'h's.

kind. 'Those are the kind of numbers that easily solve the mystery ...' (*New York Daily News*). There should be what grammarians call concord between *kind* and *kinds* and their antecedents. Just as we say 'this hat' but 'those hats', so the writer above should have said, 'Those are the kinds of numbers' or 'This is the kind of number'. Shakespeare, for what it's worth, didn't always observe the distinction. In *King Lear* he wrote: 'These kind of knaves'.

kith and kin. Your kin are your relatives. Your kith are your relatives and acquaintances. Individually the words are antiquated. Together they are redundant and hackneyed.

knot. 'The yacht was doing about nine knots an hour, according to Mr Starr' (*The New York Times*). Because *knot* means nautical miles an hour, the time element is implicit in it. The sentence above is telling us that the yacht was progressing at a speed of nine nautical miles an hour an hour. Either delete 'an hour' or change 'knots' to 'nautical miles'.

koala bears is wrong. Koalas are marsupials, not bears. Just call them koalas.

krona, krone. The currencies of the Scandinavian nations cause occasional confusion, as in this *Times* headline: 'Sweden devalues kroner by 10 per cent'. The Swedes call it a *krona* (plural *kronor*). In Denmark and Norway it is a *krone* (plural *kroner*). In Iceland it is also a *krona*, but the plural is *kronur*.

krone. See KRONA, KRONE.

Krugerrand. Often misspelled, as here: 'The premium on Krugerands was just over 3 per cent' (*Guardian*). Note the two 'r's in the middle.

kudos. 'He did not feel he had received the kudos that were his due' (*Washington Post*). *Kudos*, a Greek word meaning fame or glory, is singular. Thus it should be 'the kudos that was his due', which rather helps to expose the word as the pompous pretender that it is. There is no such thing, incidentally, as one kudo.

◉ L ◉

languid, limpid. Not to be confused. *Limpid* means clear, calm, untroubled ('a limpid stream'). It has nothing to do with being limp or listless – meanings that are covered by *languid*.

last, past, latest. Various authorities have issued various strictures against using *last* when you mean *latest*. Generally speaking, *last* should not be used when it might be interpreted as meaning final, as in 'the last issue of the newspaper' when you mean 'the latest issue'. The chances of ambiguity, however, are probably not as great as some authorities would have us believe, and in any case the choice of word is dictated as often by idiom as by sense. We must, for instance, say, 'I last saw him a week ago' or 'I spoke to him last night', even when there is no suggestion of it being a final meeting. Some newspapers make a similar distinction between *last* and *past*, though here the likelihood of confusion can generously be called remote.

latest. See LAST, PAST, LATEST.

latter. See FORMER, LATTER.

laudable, laudatory. Occasionally confused. *Laudable* means deserving praise. *Laudatory* means expressing praise.

laudatory. See LAUDABLE, LAUDATORY.

lay, lie. A constant source of errors. There are no simple rules for this pair. You must either commit their forms to memory or avoid them altogether. The forms are:

	lay	*lie*
Present:	I lay the book on the table.	I lie down; I am lying down.
Past:	Yesterday I laid the book on the table.	Last night I lay down to sleep.
Present perfect:	I have already laid the book on the table.	I have lain in bed all day.

The most common type of error is to say: 'If you're not feeling well, go upstairs and lay down'. It should be 'lie down'.

lectern, podium, dais, rostrum. The first two are frequently confused. A lectern is the stand on which a speaker places his notes. A podium is the raised platform on which he and the lectern stand. A podium can hold only one person. A platform for several people is a dais. A rostrum is any platform; it may be designed for one speaker or for several.

legend, legendary. Lytton Strachey described Florence Nightingale as 'a living legend in her own lifetime' (as opposed, apparently, to a dead legend in her own lifetime) and thereby gave the world a cliché it could do without. Properly, a legend is a story that may have some basis in fact, but is mostly fanciful. King Arthur and Robin Hood are legendary figures. The word can be fairly extended to those people or things whose fame is such as to inspire myths (Babe Ruth, Rolls-Royces), but the word is often used far too loosely, as here: 'Doctors call it Munchhausen's syndrome, after the legendary ... Baron Hieronymous Karl Friedrich von Munchhausen, who spun fantastic and exaggerated stories about his experiences as a German cavalry officer ...' (*The New York Times*). To attach the word to a man whose history is well documented and whose fame exists almost exclusively within medical circles is to use it loosely.

legendary. See LEGEND, LEGENDARY.

lend, loan. *Loan* as a verb ('He loaned me some money') is common in America, probably because *lent* sounds affected to most American ears, and is appearing increasingly in Britain as here: 'They have agreed to loan the fund more than $4,000 million' (*The Times*). However, most British authorities and two leading American ones (Bernstein and *The American Heritage Dictionary*) continue to urge that the usage be resisted.

less. See FEWER, LESS.

level, mark are often empty words. 'Share prices once again fell below the 600 level' (*Guardian*) says no more than 'fell below 600'. Similarly *mark*, as in 'This year attendances have been hovering around the 25,000 mark' (*Sunday Times*). Make it 'hovering around 25,000'.

liable, likely, apt, prone. All four indicate probability, but there are distinctions worth noting. *Apt* is better reserved for general probabilities ('It is apt to snow in January') and *likely* for specific ones ('It is likely to snow today'). *Liable* and *prone* are better used to indicate a probability arising as a regrettable consequence: 'People who drink too much are prone to fall down'; 'If you don't pay your taxes, you are liable to get caught'. Fowler says that *prone* should apply only to people, but he appears to be alone in this view and the 1982 *Concise Oxford Dictionary* cites 'strike-prone industries' as an acceptable usage.

A separate problem with *likely*, more common in America than elsewhere, is seen in this sentence: 'Cable experts say the agreement will likely strengthen the company's position' (*Washington Post*). When used as an adverb, *likely* needs to be accompanied by a 'very', 'quite', 'more', or 'most'. Thus the sentence should say 'will very likely strengthen'. A greater improvement still would be to rework the phrase entirely: 'Cable experts say the agreement is likely to strengthen the company's position'. (See also INCLINE.)

licence, license. In British usage the first is the noun, the second the verb ('a licence to sell wines and spirits' but 'licensed premises'). In America *license* is preferred for both noun and verb, although with the exception of 'practice' (which see) the distinction is elsewhere preserved, as in device/devise, advice/advise and prophecy/prophesy.

license. See LICENCE, LICENSE.

lie. See LAY, LIE.

lifelong. 'Jesse Bishop was a lifelong drug addict who had spent 20 of his 46 years in prison' (*Guardian*). You might be a lifelong resident of New York or a lifelong church-goer or, at a stretch, a lifelong lover of music. But unless the unfortunate Mr Bishop had turned to drugs at a remarkably early age, *lifelong* is much too literal a word to describe his addiction.

lighted, lit. Either is correct. *Lighted*, however, is more usual when the word is being used as an adjective ('a lighted torch').

light years. 'So protracted have the discussions been that their progress should almost be measured not in years but in light years' (*Guardian*).

Though the intention above was obviously facetious, it is as well to remember that light years are a measure of distance, not time.

like, as. Problems often arise in choosing between *like* and *as*. Here are two examples, both from *The New York Times* and both wrong: 'Advertising agencies may appear as [make it *like*] homespun enterprises to the American public ...'; 'On the surface it looks like [*as if*] all of the parties are preparing for serious bargaining'.

The rule is, on the face of it, simple: *as* and *as if* are always followed by a verb; *like* never is. Therefore we would say, 'He plays tennis like an expert' (no verb after *like*), but, 'He plays tennis as if his life depended on it' (verb *depended*).

Although that is the rule, there may be times when you wish to suspend it. Except in the most formal writing, sentences like the one you are now reading and the two that follow should not be considered objectionable: 'She looks just like her mother used to'; 'He can't dance like he used to'. There is also one apparent inconsistency in the rule in that *like* may be used when it comes between 'feel' and an '-ing' verb: 'He felt like walking'; 'I feel like going abroad this year'.

A separate problem with *like* is that it often leads writers to make false comparisons, as here: 'Like the Prime Minister, his opposition to increased public spending is fierce' (*Daily Telegraph*). The writer has inadvertently likened 'Prime Minister' to 'opposition'. In order to liken person with person, the sentence needs to be recast: 'Like the Prime Minister, he is fiercely opposed to increased public spending', or words to that effect. Phythian cites this example: 'It is believed that this strike, like last year, could go on for several weeks'. As written, the sentence is telling us that last year could go on for several weeks. Make it 'this strike, like last year's ...'.

likely. See LIABLE, LIKELY, APT, PRONE.

limit means constrained, set within bounds. Unless there is the idea of a limit being imposed, the word is being used loosely, as it was here: 'Information about his early life is limited' (cited by Fowler). It should not be used as a simple synonym for small, brief, rare, meagre or other more precise words.

limpid. See LANGUID, LIMPID.

lingua franca. See JARGON, ARGOT, LINGUA FRANCA.

link together. See JOIN TOGETHER, LINK TOGETHER.

lion's share is better avoided unless there is some suggestion of a greedy or selfish accumulation, a sense not intended here: 'The Territory, which controls the lion's share of Australia's high-grade uranium reserves ...' (*Australian*).

liquefy. Frequently misspelled, as here: 'Indonesia intends to double its exports of liquified gas to Japan' (*The Times*).

lit. See LIGHTED, LIT.

literally. All too often used as a kind of disclaimer by writers who mean – literally – the opposite of what they're saying. The result is generally painful: 'Hetzel was literally born with a butcher's knife in his mouth' (*Chicago Tribune*); 'After a slow start, they literally sliced up the Wildcats with their stunning last-half onslaught' (*San Francisco Chronicle*); 'Our eyes were literally pinned to the curtains' (cited by Fowler).

It shouldn't need saying, but if you don't wish to be taken literally, don't use *literally*. The word means actually, not figuratively. It is acceptable only when it serves to show that an expression usually used metaphorically is to be taken at its word, as in: 'He literally died laughing'.

livid. There is an uneasy compromise between the two meanings of the word. Originally *livid* indicated a bluish, leaden shade of the sort associated with bruising. It has since been extended to mean furious and argumentative, and in that sense is now well established. But the word has nothing to do with redness, as is often assumed, or with brightness, as was apparently thought here: 'For the sun room she chose a bold, almost livid, array of patterns and textures' (*Chicago Tribune*). Unless the sun room was decorated in a dullish blue, the word the writer wanted was 'vivid'.

loan. See LEND, LOAN.

local residents. 'The proposals have upset many local residents' (*Guardian*). Residents generally are local.

luxuriant, luxurious. The words are not interchangeable, though the meanings sometimes overlap. *Luxuriant* indicates profuse growth ('luxuriant hair'). *Luxurious* means sumptuous and expensive ('a luxurious house'). A luxuriant carpet is a shaggy one. A luxurious carpet is a very expensive one.

luxurious. See LUXURIANT, LUXURIOUS.

◦ **M** ◦

major. On the day in 1982 that *The New York Times* was telling its readers about a major initiative, a major undertaking, a major speech, two major changes, a major operation and a major cause, *The Times* of London was offering its readers a major scandal, a major change, two major improvements and two major steps, a major proposal, a major source of profits and a major refurbishment. *Major*, it seems, has become a major word. Generally imprecise, frequently fatuous and always grossly overworked, it is in almost every instance better replaced by a more expressive term.

majority, like *major*, has been wearied by overuse, particularly in the expression 'the vast majority of', as in the three following examples, all from authorities: 'The vast majority of conditional sentences ...' (Partridge); 'In the vast majority of instances ...' (Bernstein); 'The vast majority of such mistakes ...' (Fowler). Even when written by the most discriminating writers, 'the vast majority of' seldom says more in four words than 'most' says in one.

Majority should be reserved for describing the larger of two clearly divisible things, as in 'The majority of the members voted for the resolution'. But even then a more specific description is usually better: 52 per cent, almost two thirds, more than 70 per cent, etc. When there is no sense of a clear contrast with a minority (as in 'The majority of his spare time was spent reading'), *majority* is better avoided.

marginal is unobjectionable when used to describe something falling near a lower limit ('a marginal profit'). But it is a poor choice when all you mean is small or slight, as it was here: 'There has been a marginal improvement in relations between police and blacks in the community' (*Guardian*).

mark. See LEVEL, MARK.

masterful, masterly. Most authorities continue to insist that we observe a distinction between these two – namely that *masterly* should apply to that which is adroit and expert and *masterful* to that which is imperious and domineering. So in the following quotation *masterly* would have been the better word: 'Leroy (Satchel) Paige, a masterful pitcher and baseball showman ...' (*Washington Post*). There are two difficulties with that argument. The first is that none of the leading dictionaries insist on the distinction and most don't even indicate that such a distinction exists. The second is that *masterly* makes a clumsy adverb. Although it is grammatically correct to write, 'He swims masterly' or even 'He swims masterlily', who would want to? *Masterly* should perhaps be your first choice when you mean in the manner of a master, but to insist on it at the expense of euphony is to be overfussy.

masterly. See MASTERFUL, MASTERLY.

material. See GERMANE, RELEVANT, MATERIAL.

materialize is usually no more than a pompous synonym for occur, develop or happen. If the urge to use it is irresistible, at least try to ensure that it is not qualifying the wrong noun, as it was here: 'Hopes of an improvement in the second half of the year have not materialized' (*The Times*). The hopes had not been realized; what had not materialized was the improvement.

may. See CAN, MAY.

me. See I, ME.

mean, median, average. Imagine that we have five people with IQs of 100, 110, 120, 130 and 150. The average IQ would be the sum of the IQs divided by the number of people – in this case 122. The mean IQ would be the number falling midway between the high of 150 and low of 100 – or 125. Both average and mean are notional numbers. they needn't correspond (and in this case don't) to any actual IQs. The median, however, is the actual number that falls midway in a given series. In this case it is 120 because there are two numbers that are higher and two that are lower. Except in technical writing, *mean* and *median* are almost always better avoided because hardly anyone will know what you are really talking about.

media. 'Is the media – tnat offensive word – being fair?' (*The New York Times*). One medium, two media. See DATA.

median. See MEAN, MEDIAN, AVERAGE.

mediate. See ARBITRATE, MEDIATE.

metal, mettle. What Samuel Johnson gave the world in lexicography, he sometimes took away in spelling. It is him we can thank for the fact that we have 'deign' but 'disdain', 'moveable' but 'immovable', and 'deceit' but 'receipt', among many others. With *metal* and *mettle*, however, his inconsistency of spelling was intentional. Though both come from the Greek *metallon* (meaning 'a mine') and historically were often spelled the same, their meanings today are normally distinguished, as Johnson intended them to be. *Metal*, of course, describes one of the basic elements, such as gold, silver or copper. *Mettle* means courage or spirit. To be on your mettle is to show the world that you are ready to do your best. A common misspelling is seen here: 'Market conditions have put the hoteliers on their metal' (*Observer*).

metaphors. Enough has been written on the perils of mixed metaphors that it probably requires no more comment than to say that constructions such as the following are profoundly bad: 'This is a virgin field pregnant with possibilities' (cited by Fowler); 'Yet the President has backed him to the hilt every time the chips were down' (cited by Bernstein). The difficulty with such sentences usually is not so much that they mix metaphors as that they mix clichés. When neither of the metaphors in a sentence is hackneyed, you might just get away with it – as Shakespeare clearly did when he wrote, 'Or to take arms against a sea of troubles'.

It should also be noted that it isn't necessary to have two metaphors to botch a sentence. One will do if it is sufficiently inappropriate, as it was here: 'Indiana, ranked the No. 1 swimming power in the nation, walked away with the Big Ten championships tonight' (Associated Press).

meticulous. 'The story has been published in meticulously researched weekly parts ...' (*Observer*). *Meticulous* does not merely mean careful or thorough; it means fussily thorough and overcareful. Correctly used, it has a pejorative tone. The word today is so often misused by respected writers (the example above comes from Germaine Greer) that to object is itself perhaps a somewhat meticulous act. Meanings change and it is usually futile and occasionally retrograde to try to stand in their way. But there are at least two reasons to regard *meticulously* meticulously. First, because the earlier meaning is so obviously contrary to the meaning often intended, it is subject to misinterpretation. More importantly, there is no need for the word in its broader sense. In the example above, Ms Greer might have chosen in its stead carefully, scrupulously, thoroughly, painstakingly, punctiliously or any of a score of other words. In its earlier sense only fastidious begins to approach it in meaning. Why then debase it?

mettle. See METAL, METTLE.

militate, mitigate. Often confused. To militate is to operate against or, much more rarely, for something: 'The news of the scandal militated against his election prospects'. To mitigate means to assuage, soften, make more endurable: 'His apology mitigated the insult'. *Mitigate against* frequently appears and is always wrong.

millennium. The plural can be *millennia* or *millenniums*. In either case note the double 'n'.

minimize. 'He minimized speculation that a boardroom reshuffle was on the way' (*Observer*). *Minimize* does not mean to play down or depreciate. It means to reduce to an absolute minimum.

minuscule. Frequently misspelled, as here: 'It is a market which was miniscule only five years ago' (*Guardian*). Think of *minus*, not *mini-*.

minute detail. Almost always redundant: 'The cube will be split into little pieces and its components examined in minute detail' (*Sunday Times*). Delete *minute*.

mishap. Dictionaries generally define *mishap* as an unlucky accident, but most people give it a more narrow meaning than that – and one that would rule out this headline from *The Times*: '30 die in mishap'. Used carefully, a mishap should suggest no more than a not very serious accident. It isn't possible to say at what point it becomes an inadequate description for a misfortune, but it is unlikely to involve more than superficial injuries and certainly not multiple fatalities.

mitigate. See MILITATE, MITIGATE.

modus vivendi. Although *modus vivendi* is frequently used to mean 'way of life' (which is its literal meaning), a few authorities maintain that it should describe only a truce between disputing parties pending settlement of their disagreement. The best way to avoid offending the learned or perplexing the ignorant is to find an English equivalent.

moribund. 'Problems in the still-moribund oil tanker business mean there is little sign of recovery on the horizon' (*The Times*). *Moribund* does not mean troubled or struggling or dormant, as was intended above and frequently elsewhere. It means dying, on the point of death.

motiveless. 'French police have intensified their search for the killer in the motiveless murder of a Parisian housewife and her three children yesterday' (*The Times*). *Motiveless* is an impudent word, and under English law a possibly dangerous one, in such contexts. Who is to say at an early stage of an investigation that a murder was committed without motive?

multilateral. See UNILATERAL, BILATERAL, MULTILATERAL.

mutual, common. Most authorities continue to insist, with varying degrees of conviction, that *mutual* should be reserved for describing reciprocal relationships between two or more things and not loosely applied to those things that are shared in common. Thus, if you and I like each other, we have a mutual friendship. But if you and I both like Shakespeare, we have a common admiration. The use of *mutual* in the sense of *common* has been with us since the sixteenth century and was given a much noted boost in the nineteenth with the appearance of the Dickens novel *Our Mutual Friend*. Most authorities accept it when *common* might be interpreted as a denigration ('our common friend'), but, even so, in its looser sense the word is better avoided. It is, at all events, more often than not superfluous, as here: 'They hope to arrange a mutual exchange of prisoners' (*Daily Telegraph*). An exchange of anything could hardly be other than mutual.

myself. Except when it is used for emphasis ('I'll do it myself') or reflexively ('I cut myself while shaving'), *myself* is almost always timorous. In the following two examples, the better word is inserted in parentheses: 'Give it to John or myself (me)'; 'My wife and myself (I) would just like to say ...'.

myth. See FABLE, PARABLE, ALLEGORY, MYTH.

nation. See COUNTRY, NATION.

nauseous. 'It made me feel quite nauseous' is increasingly common, especially in America. Make it *nauseated*. As Bernstein very neatly puts it, people who are nauseated are no more nauseous than people who are poisoned are poisonous.

near disaster. 'His quick thinking saved an R A F jet pilot from a near disaster' (*The Times*). Not quite. The pilot was saved from a disaster. A near disaster is what he had.

needless to say. Then why say it? Similarly fatuous is 'it goes without saying'.

neither. Writers have been curiously confounded by the word for centuries; even Samuel Johnson bungled his grammar with *neither* at least once. Things have not improved noticeably since his day, as these two sentences show: 'Neither he nor his agent were available for comment' (*Standard*); 'But maybe neither Churchill nor Chamberlain were as gullible as these remarks suggest' (*Sunday Times*). In both the verb should be 'was'.

When a *neither ... nor* conjunction is used, the verb should agree with the noun nearest it. In the examples above, the nouns nearest the verb (respectively 'agent' and 'Chamberlain') are both singular, so the verb should be as well. When the noun nearest the verb is plural, the verb should be plural: 'Neither the Prime Minister nor her ministers were available for comment'.

It should be noted that a *neither ... or* combination is always wrong, as here: '[The] movie mixes horror with science fiction to make something that is fun as neither one thing or the other' (*The New York Times*). Make it *nor*. The following sentence makes the same error and the additional one of failing to provide a grammatical balance between the *neither* phrase and the *nor* phrase: 'Borrowing which allows a country to live beyond its means serves neither the interests of the borrower or the financial community' (*The Times*). Make it 'serves the interests of neither the borrower nor the financial community'. (For a fuller discussion of the problem, see BOTH ... AND.)

When *neither* is used on its own without the *nor*, the verb should always be singular: 'Neither of the men was ready'; 'Neither of us is hungry'.

nemesis. 'Instead, the unions directed their wrath toward another nemesis, the European Community's Executive Commission ...' (*Time*). This will come as a blow to thousands of sportswriters, and at least one writer at *Time* magazine, but a nemesis (from Nemesis, the Greek goddess of vengeance) is one who extracts retributive justice or is utterly unbeatable, and not merely a rival of long standing.

new. 'New chairman named at Weir Group' (*Financial Times* headline); 'Medical briefing: the first in an occasional series on new developments in the sciences' (*Times* headline); 'The search for new breakthroughs seems to have spurred extra spending in recent years' (*Newsweek*). As an adjective, *new* is frequently superfluous. The Weir Group would hardly be appointing an old chairman, nor scientists searching for old breakthroughs, nor *The Times*, let us hope, running a series on old developments in the sciences. In each instance it could be deleted without loss.

no. See YES, NO.

nobody. See NUMBER (4).

noisome has nothing to do with noise or noisiness. It is related to *annoy* and means offensive or objectionable and is most often used to describe unpleasant smells.

none. The widely held belief that *none* must always be singular is a myth. Since Fowler, Bernstein, Howard, Gowers, Partridge, the Evanses, the Morrises, Follett, *The Oxford English Dictionary*, *The American Heritage*, *Random House* and *Webster's New World* dictionaries and many others have already made this point, I do not suppose that the addition of my own small voice to the chorus will make a great deal of difference.

Whether you treat *none* as a singular or a plural, you should at least be consistent throughout the sentence, as this writer was not:

'None of her friends, she says, would describe themselves as a feminist' (*Guardian*). Make it either 'would describe themselves as feminists' or 'would describe herself as a feminist'.

A more notable inconsistency, if only because it comes from a respected authority, is seen here: 'The total vocabulary of English is immense and runs to about half a million items. None of us as individuals, of course, knows more than a fairly limited number of these, and uses even less ...' (Quirk, *The Use of English*). 'None of us ... uses even less'? Though the sense of the sentence is clear enough in the context, grammatically it is telling us that nobody uses fewer words than he knows – which is, unfortunately, the opposite of what the author intended. It would be better, I think, if we made it 'and we use even less' (and better still if we made it 'and we use even fewer').

non sequitur is the Latin for 'it does not follow' and means the combination of two or more unrelated statements. Non sequiturs are most commonly encountered in American newspapers in sentences like the following (which was also cited under *dangling modifiers*): 'Slim, of medium height and with sharp features, Mr Smith's technical skills are combined with strong leadership qualities' (*The New York Times*). What, we might ask, do Mr Smith's height and features have to do with his leadership qualities? The answer, of course, is not a damn thing. When non sequiturs are not intrusive and annoying, they are often just absurd, as here: 'Dyson's catch of Clarke was unbelievable, the best catch I've seen. And the one before it was just as good' (*Sydney Daily Telegraph*, cited in *Punch*).

no one. See NUMBER (4).

normalcy is widely, and wrongly, believed to have been coined by Warren G. Harding, the American president. It is in fact much older. Although most dictionaries accept it as standard, it is still derided by many authorities, who suggest *normality* instead.

not. Sometimes when writers invert the normal word order of a sentence to place greater emphasis on *not*, they present the reader with a false parenthesis. Consider this sentence by John Simon in *Paradigms Lost*: 'Could not that lingua franca be, not Esperanto, Volupük, or even English, but humour?' As punctuated, 'not Esperanto, Volupük, or even English' is parenthetical. But if we deleted it (as we should be able to do with all parenthetical expressions, including this one), the sentence would say: 'Could not that lingua franca be but humour?' The first comma should be removed. Except when the sentiment is pithy ('Death be not proud') such sentences are usually clumsy, which may account for the urge to embellish them with unnecessary punctuation.

not all. 'For some time now tales have been circulating that all was not well in the Goldsmith empire' (*The Times*). What the writer really meant was that not all was well in the empire, not that everything was unwell. The authorities are curiously, and almost unanimously, tolerant on this point. The Evanses are rather vehement about it: 'Distinctions such as this, between *all is not* and *not all is*, appeal to a fictitious logic and seem to have been invented for the purpose of proving other people in the wrong. They are not good for much else'.

I'm afraid the authorities and I are at odds here – or, as the Evanses might put it, all of us don't agree. It seems to me difficult to justify a sentence that so blatantly contradicts what it means to say, especially when the solution is as simple a matter as moving the *not* back two places. Setting aside any considerations of grammatical tidiness and rectitude, if we accept the Evanses' position, how do we make ourselves clear when we really do mean that all is not well? There are a few expressions that we must accept as idiomatic ('All is not lost', 'All that glisters is not gold'), but on the whole I think the construction is better avoided. Certainly I wouldn't want to have to defend the New York clothing store that advertised: 'All items not on sale' (cited by William Safire in *The New York Times*).

not only ... but also. The rule of correlative conjunctions (discussed under BOTH ... AND) applies equally here. That is, there should be a grammatical balance in the sentence. Thus, 'Not only does the fall in the birth-rate vary from city to city but also from area to area' (cited by Phythian) should be: 'The fall in the birth-rate varies not only from city to city but also from area to area'.

not so much is often followed by 'but' when the word should be 'as', as here: 'He was not so much a comic actor, consciously presenting an amusing part, but [make it as] a real comedian ...' (J. B. Priestley, cited by Partridge).

number. Errors of number – the failure to maintain agreement between the subject and verb in a sentence – are probably the most common grammatical fault in English and often the least excusable. In a language where so much is so complicated, the rule is gratifyingly simple: a singular subject takes a singular verb and a plural subject takes a plural verb. As Bernstein says, anyone who can distinguish between one and more than one shouldn't find that too sophisticated a challenge. Yet errors abound – even, as we shall see, among those who should know better. Many of the causes of errors are treated separately throughout the book, but five in particular are worth noting here:

1. *Errors involving 'and'.* When two nouns or pronouns joined by *and* form a compound subject, a plural verb is required. 'Impatience and anger in political and editorial circles has been sharply mounting ...' (*Los Angeles Times*). Make it 'have'. 'She told the meeting that the disorder and despair of the Conservative Party was not self-evident' (*The Times*). Make it 'were'.

The error is especially common when the normal subject-verb order is reversed, as here: 'Why, you may ask, is correct speech and writing important, as long as the writing is clear?' (Simon, *Paradigms Lost*). Speech and writing 'are' important.

Simon might argue – indeed, he would have to – that 'speech' and 'writing' are so closely related that they form a single idea. When that is the case a singular verb is unobjectionable. But such exceptions are better kept for things that are routinely combined – fish and chips, ham and eggs, law and order, the long and the short of it, etc. – and even then a plural verb would not be wrong.

2. *Errors involving 'or'.* Whereas *and* draws diverse elements together, *or* keeps them separate. When all the elements are singular, the verb should be singular too. Thus this sentence is wrong: 'A nod, wink or even a discreet tug of the ear aren't [make it 'isn't'] going to be the only sign language at the auction ...' (*Observer*). When all the elements are plural, the verb should be plural. When there is a mixture of singulars and plurals, the rule is to make the verb agree with the noun or pronoun nearest it. Consider: 'No photographs or television footage have been transmitted from the fleet for almost a week' (*The New York Times*). Because the nearest noun (footage) is singular, the verb should be 'has'. Had the two nouns been reversed, 'have' would have been correct.

The need to maintain agreement can sometimes lead to awkward constructions, particularly with pronouns. 'Is he or we wrong?' is grammatically perfect but perfectly awful. The solution would be to recast the sentence: 'Is he wrong or are we?'

A final point to note is that *or* influences not only the verb, but also subsequent nouns and pronouns. In the following sentence the correct forms are given in parentheses: 'While Paris, Mexico City, Hong Kong or Munich have (has) shown how their (its) underground systems (system) can become part of the pride of their (its) city ...' (*Observer*). A better alternative with that sentence, however, would be to change the *or* to *and* and leave the rest of it as it is.

3. *Errors caused by failure to keep track of antecedents.* Few people, it sometimes seems, have shorter attention spans than the average writer. All too often he will confidently set out with a plural or singular noun, become distracted by three or four intervening words and finish with a verb of the opposite number. Such was the case in each of the following (the correct forms are given in parentheses): 'Bank mortgages, which now account for most expensive property, is (are) not included in the figures ...' (*The Times*); 'The pressure of living and working on board 24 hours a day have (has) led to some strained relationships' (*Observer*); 'The incident demonstrates the reluctance with which some requests for interviews with ministers and senior officials is (are) met' (*The Times*).

Occasionally the writer does not even have the excuse of intervening matter: 'Meet Allan and Sondra Gotlieb, whose official titles may cause glazed looks but whose frankness have made them among the most popular, and unusual, diplomats in Washington' (*The New York Times*). Frankness 'have'?

And sometimes the intervening matter is so clearly unconnected with the main clause that the error is startling – all the more so when it is committed by as careful a user as Philip Howard: 'Populist (and its generic class of politics, populism) have recently been adopted as vogue words in British politics ...' (from *New Words for Old*). Make it 'has recently been adopted as a vogue word'. For a discussion, see PARENTHESES in the appendix.

4. *Errors involving personal pronouns.* This is a common type and one that points up the inadequacies both of English and of those who use it. Consider. 'If someone is learning a language for their job ...' (*Financial Times*). The problem is that the singular 'someone' and singular 'is' are being attached to the plural 'their'. Grammatically it is equivalent to saying 'No one were there' or 'They is studying French'.

The convention is to make the second pronoun 'his': 'If someone is learning a language for his job ...'. The obvious shortcoming is that this slights women. To avoid offending either them or grammar, you could make it 'his or her job', which is often cumbersome, or you could recast the sentence with a plural subject: 'People who are learning a language for their job ...'. I recommend recasting.

Too strict an application of the rule can result in incongruities – a point that evidently occurred to Philip Howard when he penned the following sentence in *Words Fail Me*: 'Nobody pretends any more (if they ever did) that economics is an exact science'. 'If they ever did' is strictly incorrect, but to change it to 'if he ever did' would unbalance the sense of the sentence. One way of preserving the grammar would be to make the subject plural: 'Few people pretend any more ...'. Another would be to replace 'they' with a singular pronoun: 'Nobody pretends any more (if anyone ever did) that economics is an exact science'. These solutions are not perhaps entirely satisfactory – but then neither, I think, is a grammatical error.

Whichever tack you take, you should at least be consistent throughout the sentence. Here is one in which the writer went to some lengths to get his pronouns right before abruptly self-destructing just short of home: 'Anyone who does confess to being a Sedaka fan does so with the guarded reluctance of one edging out of the closet, fearing he or she will be made immediate targets of fun' (*Sunday Times*). It should be 'an immediate target of fun'.

5. *Errors involving the word 'number'*. There is frequent confusion over whether to use a plural or singular verb with the noun *number*. Both of the following examples come from the same issue of *The Times*. Both are wrong. 'Mr Isaacs said a substantial number of households was inhabited today not by the conventional family group, but by single tenants'; 'A small, but increasing number of individuals is apparently buying secondhand British Rail coaches'. There is an easy way out of the confusion. Always make it 'The number was ...' but 'A number were ...'. The same rule applies to TOTAL.

oblivious. Both Fowler and Partridge insist that *oblivious* can mean only forgetful; you cannot be oblivious of something that you were not in the first place aware of. But in its broader sense of merely being unaware or impervious or unconscious, *oblivious* is now accepted by most dictionaries.

obsolescent. See OBSOLETE, OBSOLESCENT.

obsolete, obsolescent. Things that are no longer used or needed are *obsolete*. Things that are becoming obsolete are *obsolescent*.

obviate does not mean reduce, as is sometimes thought: 'A total re-design of the system should obviate complaints about its reliability' (*The Times*). It means to make unnecessary.

occur, take place. *Take place* is better reserved for scheduled events. When what is being described is accidental, *occur* is the better word, as it would have been here: 'The accident took place in driving rain' (*Guardian*).

oculist. See OPHTHALMOLOGIST, OCULIST, OPTOMETRIST, OP-TICIAN.

on, upon. Although some journalists think there is, or ought to be, a distinction between these two, there isn't. The choice is sometimes dictated by idiom ('upon my word', 'on no account'), but in all other instances it is a matter of preference.

one. 'The makers claim that one in 14 people in the world are following the exploits of this new hero' (*Sunday Times*). In such constructions *one* should be singular. In effect the sentence is saying: 'Out of every 14 people in the world, one is following the exploits of this new hero' A slightly trickier case appears here: 'An estimated one in three house-holders who are entitled to rate rebates are not claiming' (*The Times*). The first 'are' is correct, but the second is wrong. Again, it may help to invert the sentence: 'Of those householders who are entitled to rate rebates, one in every three is not claiming'.

one another. See EACH OTHER, ONE ANOTHER.

one of the, one of those. The problem here is similar to that discussed in the previous entry, but with the difference that here *one* does not govern the verb. Consider: 'Nott is actually one of those rare politicians who really doesn't mind what he says' (*Observer*). The operative word here is not *one* but *those*, as can be seen by inverting the sentence: 'Of those politicians who do not [not 'does not'] mind what they say, Nott is one'.

The mistake is a common one. Even Fowler makes it in his *Dictionary of Modern English Usage* when he writes: 'Prestige is one of the few words that has had an experience opposite to that described in "Worsened Words"'. It should be 'have had'. Just sixty pages earlier Fowler calls the error a frequent blunder. Which only goes to show.

It should also be noted that *one of the* is often verbose, as here: 'One of the reasons for all the excitement ...' (*Sunday Telegraph*); 'One of the members said he would almost certainly abstain' (*Guardian*). Why not simply make it 'one reason' and 'one member'?

one or more is plural. 'Inside each folder is one or more sheets of information' (cited by Bernstein) should be 'are one or more'.

only. Most of us when speaking, and too many of us when writing, are not notably discriminating about the positioning of *only* in sentences. In general, *only* ought to be attached to the word or phrase it is modifying and not set adrift, as here: 'The A Class bus only ran on Sundays' (*Observer*). As written, the sentence suggests that on other days of the week the bus did something else – perhaps flew? The writer would better have said that the bus 'ran only on Sundays' or 'on Sundays only'. The versatility of *only* can be seen in the fact that she might have placed it in any of five positions, four of which would have given the sentence quite separate meanings.

Oftentimes clarity and idiom are better served by bringing *only* to a more forward position ('This will only take a minute'; 'The victory can only be called a miracle'). But while those considerations might grant us some latitude in the positioning of *only*, they shouldn't excuse ambiguity or sloppiness.

onstream. A pretentious variant for 'begin' or 'open', as in 'The factory will come onstream in 1983' (*Guardian*).

ophthalmologist, oculist, optometrist, optician. *Ophthalmologist* can frequently be seen misspelled – including on the windows of one very upmarket optical shop on Sloane Street in London. Note that it begins *oph-* and not *opth-* and that the first syllable is pronounced *off*, not *op*. Thus it is similar in both pronunciation and spelling to diphtheria, diphthong and naphtha, all of which are frequently misspelled and more frequently mispronounced.

Ophthalmologist and *oculist* both describe doctors who specialize in diseases of the eye. An *optometrist* is one who is trained to test eyes but is not a doctor. An *optician* is one who makes or sells corrective lenses.

opine. Quaint, stilted and better avoided.

opposite. See CONTRARY, CONVERSE, OPPOSITE, REVERSE.

opt, choose. Safire suggests that *opt* would be a more expressive word if we used it only to describe impulsive choices, and he is right. But it must be said that none of the leading dictionaries note or encourage such a distinction.

optician. See OPHTHALMOLOGIST, OCULIST, OPTOMETRIST, OPTICIAN.

optimistic, pessimistic. Both words are better used to describe a general outlook rather than a specific view, particularly with regard to the inconsequential. 'He was optimistic that he would find the missing book' would be better as 'was hopeful' or 'was confident'.

optimum does not mean greatest or fastest or biggest, as is sometimes thought. It describes the point at which conflicting considerations are reconciled. The optimum take-off speed of an aircraft, for instance, is the fastest speed at which it can take off without becoming unsafe or uncomfortable or wasteful of fuel.

optometrist. See OPHTHALMOLOGIST, OCULIST, OPTOMETRIST, OPTICIAN.

or. A frequent source of errors, even sometimes among the authorities, as here: 'Short words rather than long ones are naturally used in headlines: "investigation" becomes "probe"; "questioning" or "interrogation" become "quiz"; "examination" becomes "test" ' (Frederick T. Wood, *Current English Usage*). It should be 'becomes' all three times. For a discussion, see NUMBER (2).

oral, verbal. 'The 1960 understanding . . . was a verbal understanding that was never written down' (*The New York Times*). Because *oral* can apply only to the spoken word, it would have been a better choice. *Verbal*, which can apply to both spoken and written words, is more usefully employed to distinguish between words and gestures or between words and substance. In the example above, however, neither word is necessary. It would be enough to say, 'The 1960 understanding was never written down'.

orientate is not incorrect, but it has nothing to recommend it over the shorter and simpler *orient*.

output. See INPUT, OUTPUT.

over. The notion that *over* is incorrect for 'more than' (as in 'over 300 people were present') is a widely held superstition. The stricture has been traced to Ambrose Bierce's *Write It Right* (1909), a usage book teeming with quirks and quiddities, most of which have since been discarded. There is no harm in preferring 'more than', but also no basis for insisting on it.

overly. 'Even granting that some past environmental arguments have been overly alarmist, the evidence against acid rain cannot be ignored' (*Chicago Tribune*). Making *over* into *overly* is a little like turning 'soon' into 'soonly'. Adding an *-ly* does nothing for *over* that it couldn't already do before. The convention in America is to attach *over* directly to the word it is modifying (overalarmist, overearnest), though in Britain hyphens are often used (over-careful, over-eager). When this becomes overinelegant or even over-inelegant, the alternative is to find another adverb: 'excessively' or 'unnecessarily' or even the admirably concise 'too'.

overweening. Arrogant or presumptuous expectations are overweening ones. There is no word *overweaning*.

ozone. Those people who like to refer to fresh air as ozone indulge in an expression that is not only a cliché but also a grossly inaccurate one. Although ozone is present in the air we breathe, it is a noxious substance and in all but the smallest quantities is lethal.

◉ **P** ◉

panacea is a universal remedy, a cure for all woes, and is not properly applied to a single shortcoming, as it was here: 'One of the best panaceas for the styling similarity of many modern cars seems to be the removal of the roof' (*Observer*).

parable. See FABLE, PARABLE, ALLEGORY, MYTH.

parameter. If you need a word to describe the relationship between a diameter and its conjugate in a conic section, or the points on a crystal at which the axes intercept a given plane, or a neat way of describing an aggregation of curves that are constant in one case but are otherwise varied, then *parameter* is the very thing. In all other instances I would venture that you were merely trying to impress us, like the US government official who called his study 'Evaluation and Parameterization of Stability and Safety Performance Characteristics of Two and Three Wheeled Vehicular Toys for Riding' (cited by Bernstein, who provides this translation: 'Why Children Fall Off Bicycles'). If all you mean is boundary or limit or perimeter, don't use *parameter*.

partially. See PARTLY, PARTIALLY.

partly, partially. Although they are often interchangeable, their meanings are slightly different. *Partially* means incompletely and *partly* means in part. 'The house was made partially of brick and partially of stone' would be better as 'partly of brick and partly of stone'. A separate danger with *partly* can be seen here: 'He was partly educated at Eton' (*The Times*), which prompted more than one wag to ask, 'Which part of him?'

past. See LAST, PAST, LATEST.

past history. 'The Tristan islanders talk of their past history with great pride' (*Sunday Times*). Hopelessly redundant, as are past records, past experience, past achievements and past precedents.

pastiche. 'This provided the occasion for a successful pastiche of that great Fonda film, Twelve Angry Men' (*The Times*). A pastiche is a work inspired by a variety of sources. The word the writer was groping for here was parody.

patois. See DIALECT, PATOIS.

peaceable, peaceful. *Peaceful* means tranquil and serene. *Peaceable* is a disposition towards the state of peacefulness.

peaceful. See PEACEABLE, PEACEFUL.

pedagogue. See PEDANT, PEDAGOGUE.

pedant, pedagogue. The two are synonyms. They describe someone who makes an ostentatious show of his learning or is dogmatically fussy about rules. Some dictionaries still give pedagogue as a synonym for teacher or educator, but its pejorative sense has effectively driven out the neutral one.

per. Generally, it is better not to use Latinisms when English phrases are available. 'Ten tons a year' is better than 'ten tons per annum'. It is also generally better not to mix Latin and English, as in 'ten tons per year'. But when avoidance of the Latin would result in clumsy constructions such as 'output a man a year', don't hesitate to use *per*.

percentage, proportion. The words are used inexactly when the relationship between two numbers isn't specified. 'This drug has proved of much value in a percentage of cases' (cited by Gowers) tells us next to nothing; it could mean 2 per cent or 98 per cent. Similarly, 'a ship of large proportions' would be better replaced by 'a ship of large dimensions' or simply 'a large ship'.

perpetrate, perpetuate. Occasionally confused. To perpetrate is to commit or perform. To perpetuate is to prolong or, literally, to make perpetual. Jack the Ripper perpetrated a series of murders. Those who write about him perpetuate his notoriety.

perpetuate. See PERPETRATE, PERPETUATE.

personal, personally. When it is necessary to indicate that a person is acting on his own rather than as a spokesman or that he is addressing people individually rather than collectively, *personal* and *personally* are unobjectionable. But usually the context makes that clear and the word is used without purpose, particularly in the expression 'personal friend'. Here the writer considerately draws our attention to the gratuitous use of the word by setting it off with equally gratuitous punctuation: 'He said that he "personally" wished that Princeton had selected a less harsh penalty' (*Chicago Tribune*).

personally. See PERSONAL, PERSONALLY.

perspicacity, perspicuity. *Perspicacity* means shrewdness and applies to people ('a perspicacious judge of character'). *Perspicuity* means easily understood and applies to things ('a perspicuous explanation'). But 'shrewd' for the first and 'clear' for the second are both briefer and more widely understood.

perspicuity. See PERSPICACITY, PERSPICUITY.

persuade. See CONVINCE, PERSUADE.

perturb. See DISTURB, PERTURB.

peruse. 'Those of us who have been idly perusing the latest flock of holiday brochures ...' (*Guardian*). *Peruse* does not mean to look over. It means to read carefully. You cannot do it idly.

pessimistic. See OPTIMISTIC, PESSIMISTIC.

Philippines. Often misspelled. Note: one 'l', double 'p'. A native is a Filipino.

phrasal verbs. One of the more versatile aspects of English is its ability to give new shades of meaning to verbs by attaching adverbial particles to them to form what are called phrasal verbs. Thus we can *break up, break off, break down, break in, break into* and *break away from*, or *take to, take off, take in, take up, take down* or *take away*. Each expression conveys a nuance that would not be possible without the particle. But this capacity to grace a verb with a tail sometimes leads writers to add a particle where none is needed. Thus we get *head up*, *check out*, *lose out*, *pay off*, *try out*, *cut back*, *meet with*, *trigger off* and countless others. Sometimes such expressions, though strictly unnecessary, gain the force of idiom (*stand up*, *sit down*, *beat up*), but just as often they are merely a sign of verbosity or carelessness. In the following examples, the italicized words do nothing but consume space: 'Now the bureau proposes to sell *off* 280 acres ...' (*Time*); 'The time will be cut *down* to two hours within two years' (*Daily Telegraph*); 'A light snowfall did little to slow *down* the British advance' (*Sunday Times*).

pidgin. See C R E O L E, PIDGIN.

Pittsburgh. Often misspelled *Pittsburg* outside North America. Since 1894, when Pittsburgh refused to comply with an order by the US Board on Geographic Names that all *-burghs* in America should become *-burgs* and all *-boroughs* should become *-boros*, it has been almost the only community in the country whose name ends with a *-gh*. There are Pittsburgs in California, Kansas, Kentucky, New Hampshire, Oklahoma and Texas, but the city in Pennsylvania is exceptionally and defiantly Pittsburgh.

pity. See EMPATHY, SYMPATHY, COMPASSION, PITY, COMMISERATION.

plan ahead. '[The] keys to success are to plan ahead, to choose manageable recipes and to cook in batches' (*The New York Times*). Always tautological. Would you plan behind?

pleonasm. See TAUTOLOGY, REDUNDANCY, PLEONASM, SOLECISM.

plethora is not merely a lot, it is an excessive amount, a superabundance. For a word that is often similarly misused, see S P A T E.

plus. 'The end of the holiday season plus the fact that London banks remained closed were cited as factors contributing to the quiet trading day' (Associated Press). *Plus* is a preposition, equivalent to 'with the addition of', and not a conjunction, and therefore does not influence the number of the verb. Two and two are four, but two plus two is four. The example above should say 'was cited as a factor' or *plus* should be changed to 'and'.

podium. See LECTERN, PODIUM, DAIS, ROSTRUM.

pore, pour. Occasionally *pour* appears where *pore* is intended. As a verb, *pore* means to examine carefully ('He pored over the documents') or, more rarely, to meditate. *Pour* indicates a flow, either literally ('He poured the water down the drain') or figuratively ('The rioters poured through the streets').

position. Often a sign of verbosity. 'They now find themselves in a position where they have to make a choice' (*Daily Telegraph*) would be immeasurably better as 'They now have to make a choice'.

possible is wrongly followed by 'may' in constructions such as the following: 'It is possible that she may decide to go after all' (*Daily Telegraph*). Make it either 'It is possible that she will decide to go after all' or 'She may decide to go after all'. Together the two words are unnecessary.

pour. See PORE, POUR.

practicable. See PRACTICAL, PRACTICABLE.

practical, practicable. Anything that can be done *and* is worth doing is practical. Anything that can be done, whether or not it is worth doing, is practicable.

practically. See VIRTUALLY, PRACTICALLY.

practice, practise. 'U.S. usage ... spells both noun and verb *practise*, as with *license*' (Harry Fieldhouse, *Everyman's Good English Guide*). That is a common misconception outside North America. In the United States, *practice* is in fact always spelled with a 'c': *practice*, *practiced*, *practicing*. In British usage, the noun is spelled *practice* ('Practice makes perfect') and the verb *practise* ('You must practise your piano lessons').

practise. See PRACTICE, PRACTISE.

precautionary measure. Why not simply *precaution*?

precipitant, precipitate, precipitous. All three come from the Latin *praecipitare* ('to throw headlong'). *Precipitous* means very steep; cliff faces are precipitous. *Precipitant* and *precipitate* both indicate a headlong rush and are almost indistinguishable in meaning. But *precipitant* tends to emphasize the abruptness of the rush and *precipitate* the rashness of it. The most common error is to use *precipitous* to describe actions ('his precipitous departure from the Cabinet'). *Precipitous* can describe only physical characteristics.

precipitate. See PRECIPITANT, PRECIPITATE, PRECIPITOUS.

precipitous. See PRECIPITANT, PRECIPITATE, PRECIPITOUS.

precondition. 'There are, however, three preconditions to be met before negotiations can begin' (*Guardian*). *Pre-* adds nothing to the meaning of *condition* and should be excised. *Preplanning* is similarly superfluous.

premises. 'His business premises was raided by environmental health officers and police' (*Daily Telegraph*). *Premises* is plural. There is no such thing as a business premise.

prepositions at end of sentences. Anyone who believes that it is wrong to end a sentence with a preposition – and there are still some who do – is about a century out of touch. The 'rule' was enshrined by one Robert Lowth, an eighteenth-century Bishop of London and gentleman grammarian. In his wildly idiosyncratic but curiously influential *Short Introduction to English Grammar*, Lowth urged his readers not to end sentences with prepositions if they could decently avoid it. Too many people took him too literally and for a century and a half the notion held sway. Today, happily, it is universally condemned as a ridiculous affectation. Indeed, there are many sentences where the preposition could scarcely come anywhere but at the end: 'This bed hasn't been slept in'; 'What is the world coming to?'; 'I don't know what you are talking about'.

prescribe, proscribe. *Prescribe* means to set down as a rule or guide. *Proscribe* means to denounce or prohibit. If you get bronchitis, your doctor may prescribe antibiotics and proscribe smoking.

present, presently. Like 'current' and 'currently', these two are often vacuous, as here: 'A new factory, which is presently under construction in Manchester, will add to capacity' (*The Times*). *Presently* adds nothing and should be deleted.

presently. See PRESENT, PRESENTLY.

pressurize. 'Esso accused him of trying to pressurize the Prime Minister into bailing out his petrochemical plant ...' (*The Times*). Gases, liquids and foods can be pressurized (i.e., compacted into containers under pressure). People are pressed or pressured.

prestigious. Some writers continue to insist that *prestigious* can properly describe only that which is deceptive or illusory because the word comes from the Latin *praestigeae*, meaning 'juggler's tricks'. That meaning has in fact been dying since the early nineteenth century.

To try to defend the stricter meaning now on grounds of etymology is rather like insisting that 'silly' must, because of its derivation, mean happy and holy or that a villain is someone who works in a villa or that 'nice' should describe only those who are ignorant and un-aware. Meanings change. When those changes appear to be for the worse, we might fairly try to get in their way. But with *prestigious* that would be neither practical nor desirable. People have been broadening its sense for almost 200 years, not as an act of defiance against the grammarians, but simply because the newer meaning was felt to be needed and the older was not. Today the original sense of the word is effectively dead everywhere but in the hearts of a scattering of purists. Most dictionaries now give the broader sense of 'worthy of esteem' as the only one, including (since 1976) one of the word's last defenders, *The Concise Oxford*.

presumptive, presumptuous. The first is often used when the second is intended. *Presumptuous* means impudent and inclined to take liberties, or excessively bold and forthright. *Presumptive* means giving grounds to presume and is primarily a technical term. The wrong use is seen here: 'She considered the question with the equanimity of someone who has long since become immune to presumptive prying' (*Sunday Telegraph*). It should be *presumptuous*.

presumptuous. See PRESUMPTIVE, PRESUMPTUOUS.

prevaricate, procrastinate. Curiously, but frequently, confused. *Prevaricate* means to speak or act evasively, to stray from the truth. *Procrastinate* means to put off doing.

prevent often appears incorrectly in sentences such as this: 'They tried to prevent him leaving'. It should be: 'They tried to prevent his leaving' or 'they tried to prevent him from leaving'. (See GERUNDS (2).)

preventative is not incorrect, but *preventive* is preferred.

prima facie. See A PRIORI, PRIMA FACIE.

principal, principle. *Principle* means fundamental and is usually applied to fundamental beliefs or truths ('It's not the money, it's the principle') or to fundamental understandings ('They have signed an agreement in principle'). It is always a noun. *Principal* can be a noun meaning chief or of first importance ('He is the school's principal') or an adjective with the same meaning ('The principal reason for my going ...').

principle. See PRINCIPAL, PRINCIPLE.

prior to. See BEFORE, PRIOR TO.

pristine. '... the campaign waged by the anti-repeal forces was pristine clean' (cited by Kingsley Amis in *The State of the Language*). *Pristine* does not mean spotless, as was apparently intended above, or brand new, as is frequently intended elsewhere. It means original or primeval or in a state virtually unchanged from the original.

procrastinate. See PREVARICATE, PROCRASTINATE.

prodigal does not mean wandering or given to running away, a sense sometimes wrongly inferred from the Biblical story of the Prodigal Son. It means recklessly wasteful or extravagant.

prognosis. See DIAGNOSIS, PROGNOSIS.

prohibit. See FORBID, PROHIBIT.

prone, prostrate, recumbent, supine. *Supine* means lying face upwards (it may help to remember that a supine person is on his spine). *Prone* and *prostrate* are regarded by most authorities – but by no means all – as meaning lying face downwards. *Prostrate* should, in any case, suggest throwing oneself down, either in submission or for protection; someone who is merely asleep shouldn't be called prostrate. *Recumbent* means lying flat in any position, but, like repose, it should indicate a position of ease and comfort.

For the other sense of *prone*, see LIABLE, LIKELY, APT, PRONE.

proper nouns. Many writers are strangely at a loss when confronted with the challenge of finding a plural form for a proper noun, as in the two following examples, both from *The Times* and both wrong: 'This is the first of a new series about the Rush's'; 'The two Germanies are hoping to establish closer links at the summit'. The rule is simple. An *s* should be added to those names that will take it: the Smiths, the Browns, the Lowes, the two Germanys. Names that end in *s*, *sh*, *ch* or *x* should be given an *es*: the Foxes, the Joneses, the Rushes. The rule is invariable with Anglo-Saxon surnames, but there are a few exceptions with other proper nouns, among them *Mercuries*, *Ptolemies*, *Rockies* and *Alleghenies*.

prophecy, prophesy. The first is the noun, the second the verb: 'I prophesy war; that is my prophecy'.

prophesy. See PROPHECY, PROPHESY.

proportion. See PERCENTAGE, PROPORTION.

proscribe. See PRESCRIBE, PROSCRIBE.

prostrate. See PRONE, PROSTRATE, RECUMBENT, SUPINE.

protagonist. Literally the word means 'first actor' (from the Greek *protos* and *agonistes*) and by extension may be applied to the principal person in any affair. But it cannot properly apply to more than one person, as was thought here: 'During the anomalous decade of the 1930s the three protagonists of this book each played out important – if somewhat ephemeral – roles ...' (*The New York Times*). The word is not the opposite of *antagonist*, of which there can be any number.

Nor does it have anything to do with the Latin *pro-* (meaning 'for' or 'on behalf of'). A protagonist may champion a cause – and in practice often does – but that isn't implicit in the word.

prototype is the word for an original that serves as a model for later products of its type. Thus first prototype, experimental prototype and model prototype are all usually redundant.

proved, proven. 'Sizewell – a case not proven' (*New Scientist* headline). *Proved* is the preferred past participle, but there are two exceptions. One is in references to Scottish law, where there is a verdict of *not proven*, and the other is in the expression *proven reserves*, as in 'The company has proven reserves of 20 million barrels of oil in the Brent field'.

proven. See PROVED, PROVEN.

proverbial is wrongly used when there is no connection with a proverb, as here: 'He stuck up the proverbial two fingers' (*Daily Mail*).

provided, providing. Most authorities consider the first preferable to the second in constructions such as 'He agreed to come provided he could get the day off work', but either would be correct. 'If' is often better still.

providing. See PROVIDED, PROVIDING.

purport means to give the appearance or idea of. Two points need to be noted when using it:
  1. It should not be used passively. 'The relics are purported to come from Etruria' should be 'The relics purport to come from Etruria'.
  2. It should apply only to things or, more rarely, to a person or persons considered as a phenomenon. Fowler cites this as a legitimate use: 'The Gibeonites sent men to Joshua purporting to be ambassadors from a far country'. And he cites this as an illegitimate one: 'She purports to find a close parallel between the Aeschylean Trilogy and The Ring ...'.

purposefully. See PURPOSELY, PURPOSEFULLY.

purposely, purposefully. The first means intentionally; the second means with an objective in mind. 'He purposely nudged me' means it was no accident. 'He purposefully nudged me' means he did it for a purpose – perhaps to draw my attention to something.

put an end to is an expression to which we should do just that. Make it 'stop'.

pyrrhic victory is not, as is sometimes thought, a hollow triumph. It is one won at great cost.

quandary. Not *quandry*.

quantum. '"It gives us the opportunity to make a quantum leap in the growth of our business," he said yesterday' (*The Times*). A quantum jump is not, as is often thought, a huge one. It is almost the opposite. It describes a significant but really rather small advance from one plane to another. If we use the analogy of a man standing at the foot of a stairway, if he made a quantum leap, he would not bound to the top, but would merely hop on to the first step. Anyone who understands theoretical physics will no doubt consider that a hopelessly simplistic interpretation, but then anyone who understands theoretical physics is unlikely to misuse quantum. For the rest of us, it is enough to say that the word is much too technical to be employed casually.

query, inquiry, enquiry. A query is a single question. An inquiry or enquiry may be a single question or an extensive investigation. Either spelling is correct, but *inquiry* is preferred by most dictionaries in both Britain and America.

question, leading and **begging the.** Both expressions are commonly misunderstood. A leading question is not a challenging or hostile one, but rather the opposite. It is one designed to help the person being questioned make the desired response. A lawyer who says to a witness, 'You didn't see the murder, did you?' has asked a leading question.

Begging the question does not mean evading a straight answer, as was thought here: 'But to say that comedians don't tell spouse jokes simply because they're not married begs the question to a large extent' (*Boston Globe*). It means to use as a basis of proof something that itself needs proving. If I say that the House of Lords should be abolished because it is a worthless institution, I must first prove that it has no worth. The expression means arguing in a circle.

question mark has become an overworked embellishment of the expression 'a question hanging over', which is itself tattered from overuse. Consider: 'The case of Geoffrey Prime ... has raised a question mark over the competence of British security' (*The Times*). Would you say of a happy event that it had raised an exclamation mark over the proceedings or that a pause in negotiations had a comma hanging over them?

quite. Because *quite* means positively or completely, some authorities object to its use where it creates a redundancy, as in 'quite all right' and 'quite similar'. Such expressions are perhaps a little quaint and certainly better avoided in formal writing, but equally they could be defended as idiomatic.

quorum. The plural is *quorums*, not *quora*.

quoting in fragments is often a timid and needless affectation, as here: 'He said that profits in the second half would be "good"' (*The Times*). Quoted matter, especially when in fragments, should have some justification. When the word or words being quoted are unusual or unexpected or particularly descriptive ('It was, he said, a "lousy" performance') or are otherwise notable, the use of punctuation marks is always unobjectionable and usually advisable. But to set off a neutral and workaday word like 'good' in the example above is unwarranted. Here is a sentence in which the second set of quotation marks is as unobjectionable as the first is fatuous: 'Dietz agreed that loneliness was a "feature" of Hinckley's life but he added that studies have shown that "loneliness is as common as the common cold in winter"' (*Washington Post*).

A separate, grammatical danger of quoting in fragments is seen here: 'Although he refused to be drawn on the future of the factory, Sir Kenneth said that the hope of finding a buyer "was not out of the question"' (*The Times*). Sir Kenneth would have said, 'That *is* not out of the question', not 'That *was* not out of the question'. In quoted material, even when fragmentary, the tense must be preserved.

A final problem is the tendency of some writers to put the words of one person into the mouths of many, as here: 'Witnesses at the scene said that there was "a tremendous bang and then all hell broke loose"' (*Guardian*). The comment should be paraphrased or attributed to just one witness.

◉ R ◉

rack, wrack. 'It noted that its reserves constituted a very slender margin of safety in a world increasingly wracked by political risks' (*The Times*). *Wrack* means wreck and almost never appears except in the expression 'wrack and ruin' – which is, incidentally, both a redundancy and a cliché. *Rack*, the word intended in the quotation above, means to put under strain. The expressions are 'nerve-racking' and 'to rack one's brains'.

raining cats and dogs. No one knows what inspired this expression, but it is worth noting that in 1738, when Swift condemned it, it was already hackneyed.

rapt, wrapped. 'Rapt in thought' occasionally appears as 'wrapped in thought', which is incorrect. *Rapt* is the past participle of an extinct verb, *rap*. It means engrossed, absorbed, enraptured.

razed. 'Zurich's Autonomous Youth Centre was razed to the ground yesterday' (*The Times*). The ground is the only place that a building can be razed to. It is enough to say: 'Zurich's Autonomous Youth Centre was razed yesterday'.

razzamatazz. See RAZZMATAZZ, RAZZAMATAZZ.

razzmatazz, razzamatazz. Often misspelled, as here: 'For them the promotional razamataz is much more about holding on to what they have' (*The Times*). *The Concise Oxford* gives either of the above spellings. *The American Heritage Dictionary* curiously does not treat the word at all.

reaction is better reserved for spontaneous responses ('He reacted to the news by fainting'). It should not be used to indicate responses marked by reflection, as it was here: 'He said he could give no reaction until he had had time to consider the proposal' (*Daily Telegraph*). Response, reply or answer would be better words.

reason. A few authorities are oddly inconsistent – unreasonable even – on the uses of *reason*. Fowler, for instance, maintains that 'reason is because' is a tautology. Thus, 'The reason he went inside is because it was raining' should be 'The reason he went inside is it was raining' or, preferably, 'He went inside because it was raining'. On this Fowler is undoubtedly right. Yet he raises no objection to 'reason why', which often looks equally tautological, and in fact frequently employs the expression himself, as here: 'No doubt the reason why we substitute the definite article for the indefinite ...'. So does Gowers in *The Complete Plain Words*: 'Perhaps the reason why it is so difficult to restrain the word to its "correct" meaning ...'. The Evanses defend both 'reason why' and 'reason is because' as idiomatic, but it does bear pointing out that 'why' in the previous two quotations could be deleted without loss, just as 'the reason' could be dispensed with here: 'If they don't, great bands of shareholders will want to know the reason why' (*Daily Mail*).

rebut, refute. 'Banks refute Lever arguments' (*Times* headline, first edition); 'Banks rebut Lever arguments' (*Times* headline, second edition). The writer of the first headline, like many other people, thought that *refute* means simply to deny or oppose an allegation. He was wrong. Someone else, aware that *refute* is a contentious word and carries a more specific meaning, changed it to *rebut*. He too was quite wrong. *Refute* means to show conclusively that an allegation is wrong. *Rebut* means to disprove an allegation and to answer in kind. If I call you an uneducated bumpkin and you show me your university diploma, then you have refuted my charge. If in addition you say, 'But you, sir, are stupid beyond measure', you have rebutted it. If all you do is deny the allegation, then neither word applies.

reconstruction. 'The play is a dramatic reconstruction of what might happen when a combination of freak weather conditions threatens to flood London' (*The Times*). It shouldn't need saying, but you cannot reconstruct an event that has not yet happened. *Re-* is often prefixed to words where it adds no meaning, most notably 'recopy' and 'reduplicate'.

recumbent. See PRONE, PROSTRATE, RECUMBENT, SUPINE.

reduce. See DEPLETE, REDUCE.

redundancy. See TAUTOLOGY, REDUNDANCY, PLEONASM, SOLECISM,

refute. See REBUT, REFUTE.

regretfully, regrettably. The first means with feelings of regret: 'Regretfully they said their farewells'. The second means unfortunately: 'Regrettably I didn't have enough money to buy it'.

regrettably. See REGRETFULLY, REGRETTABLY.

reiterate. Since *iterate* means repeat, *reiterate* ought to mean re-repeat, but it doesn't. It too just means repeat. That is perhaps fortunate; otherwise the following sentence would in effect be saying re-re-repeat: 'She hopes her message to the markets, reiterated again at the weekend, will be enough to prevent the pound sliding further' (*The Times*). 'Again' is always superfluous with *re-* words (reiterate, repeat, reaffirm) and should be deleted.

relatively, like comparatively, should not be used unless there is some indication of a comparison or relationship. As often as not, the word can be removed without loss, as here: 'The group has taken the relatively bold decision to expand its interests in Nigeria' (*The Times*).

relevant. See GERMANE, RELEVANT, MATERIAL.

relieve. See ALLAY, ALLEVIATE, ASSUAGE, RELIEVE.

repel, repulse. Not to be confused. *Repulse* means to drive back: 'The army repulsed the enemy's attack'. It shouldn't be confused with *repulsive*, meaning to cause repugnance. *Repel* is the word for causing squeamishness or distaste: 'The idea of eating squid repelled her'.

replica. In art, a replica is a duplicate made by the original artist. In other contexts it means an almost exact copy – one built to the same dimensions and using the same materials. To use the word when you might better use model, miniature, copy or reproduction devalues it, as here: 'Using nothing but plastic Lego toy bricks, they have painstakingly constructed replicas of some of the world's most famous landmarks' (*Sunday Times*).

repulse. See REPEL, REPULSE.

restaurateur, not *restauranteur*.

restive. Originally the word meant balky, refusing to move or budge, but through confusion has come more and more to be used as a synonym for restless. Most dictionaries now recognize both meanings, but if the word is to have any value it should contain at least some suggestion of resistance. A crowd of protesters may grow restive upon the arrival of mounted police, but a person sleeping fitfully would be better described as restless.

revenge. See AVENGE, REVENGE.

reverse. See CONTRARY, CONVERSE, OPPOSITE, REVERSE.

revert back is always redundant: 'If no other claimant can be found, the right to the money will revert back to her' (*Daily Telegraph*). Delete *back*.

rostrum. See LECTERN, PODIUM, DAIS, ROSTRUM.

⊡ S ⊡

sacrilegious. Sometimes misspelled *sacreligious* on the mistaken assumption that *religious* is part of the word. It isn't.

salutary. See HEALTHY, HEALTHFUL, SALUTARY.

sarcasm. See IRONY, SARCASM.

scrutiny. The word is a magnet for superfluous adjectives, as here: 'Mr Shultz's activities are expected to attract close scrutiny' (*The New York Times*). *Scrutiny* means to give careful attention, so close or careful scrutiny is redundant. Bernstein, who often cautioned against the solecism, actually commits it himself in *The Careful Writer* when he says: 'Under close scrutiny, many constructions containing the word "not" make no sense ...'. In the same volume he unwittingly underlines the point by urging writers to 'scrutinize thoughtfully every phrase that eases itself almost mechanically onto the paper'. Had he followed his own advice, he no doubt would have deleted 'thoughtfully' there.

scurrilous, which is most often encountered in the expression 'a scurrilous attack', does not mean specious or disreputable, though those senses are often intended. It means grossly obscene or abusive. An attack must be exceedingly harsh to be scurrilous.

second largest and other similar comparisons often lead writers astray: 'Japan is the second largest drugs market in the world after the United States' (*The Times*). Not quite. It is the largest drugs market in the world after the United States or it is the second largest drugs market in the world.

self-confessed, as in 'a self-confessed murderer', is tautological. *Confessed* alone is enough.

sensual, sensuous. The words are only broadly synonymous. *Sensual* applies to a person's baser instincts as distinguished from reason. It should always hold connotations of sexual allure and lust. *Sensuous* was coined by Milton to avoid those connotations and to suggest instead the idea of being alive to sensations. It should be used when there is no suggestion of sexual arousal.

sensuous. See SENSUAL, SENSUOUS.

servicing. See SERVING, SERVICING.

serving, servicing. 'Cable TV could be servicing half the country within five years' (*Daily Mail*). Bulls service cows; mechanics service faulty machinery. But cable TV systems serve the country. *Servicing* is better reserved for the idea of installation and maintenance. *Serve* is the better word for describing things that are of general and continuing benefit.

shall, will. Authorities have been trying to pin down the vagaries of *shall* and *will* since the seventeenth century, and most have come a cropper. In *The King's English*, the Fowler brothers devote twenty pages to the distinctions. The gist of what they have to say is that either you understand the distinctions instinctively or you don't; that if you don't, you probably never will; and that if you do, you don't need to be told anyway.

The rule most frequently propounded is that to express simple futurity you should use *shall* in the first person and *will* in the second and third persons, and to express determination (or volition) you should do the reverse. But by that rule Churchill committed a grammatical blunder when he vowed: 'We shall fight in the fields and in the streets, we shall fight in the hills; we shall never surrender'. As did MacArthur when he said at Corregidor: 'I shall return'. As have all those who have ever sung 'We Shall Overcome'.

The simple fact is that whether you use *shall* or *will* in a given instance depends very much on your age and your birthplace and the emphasis with which you mean to express yourself. The English tend to use *shall* more frequently and more specifically than do the Scots or Irish or Americans, but even in England the distinctions are quickly fading and by no means fixed.

To try to formulate rules here would be a dangerous and perhaps impossible exercise for an Englishman. For an American, it would be folly of the first order.

shambles properly describes a scene of carnage (it was formerly a word for a slaughterhouse). We might excuse its more common sense of chaos or disorderliness ('The second act of the play was a shambles') when used conversationally or jocularly, but as a serious and considered term it is otiose when there is no suggestion of bloodshed, as here: 'The Colonial Secretary denied ... that the conference on the future of Malta had been a shambles' (cited by Fowler).

should like. 'I should have liked to have seen it' should be 'I should like to have seen it' or 'I should have liked to see it'. (For American usage read *would* for *should*.)

since. 'She gave strong support to the visions of the late Bernard Kilgore and the other executives and editors who operated the Journal and Dow Jones since World War II' (*Wall Street Journal*); 'Since April the Inland Revenue stopped giving immediate tax refunds to those who were unlucky enough to become unemployed' (*The Times*). *Since* indicates action starting at a specified time in the past and continuing up to the present. The verbs in sentences in which it appears must also indicate action that is still continuing – that is, they should be 'have operated' in the first instance and 'has stopped' in the second. As written, both sentences border on the illiterate.

situation. Residents of Britain owe a great debt to the magazine *Private Eye* for mocking the gratuitous use of *situation* into near obscurity through its Ongoing Situations column. The usage is, however, still common in the United States: 'The exchange ... had failed to be alert to the potential of a crisis situation as it developed' (*The New York Times*). Delete *situation*.

sleight of hand, not slight of hand. *Sleight*, meaning dextrous or deceptive, comes from the Old Norse *sloegdh*, and *slight*, meaning slender or frail, comes from the Old Norse *slettr*, but they have nothing else in common except their pronunciation.

solecism. See TAUTOLOGY, REDUNDANCY, PLEONASM, SOLECISM.

sometime, some time. Most often it is one word: 'They will arrive sometime tomorrow'. But when *some* is used as an adjective equivalent to 'a short' or 'a long' or 'an indefinite', it should be two words: 'The announcement was made some time ago'.

Three considerations may help you to make the distinction:

1. *Some time* as two words is usually preceded by a preposition (for some time, at some time) or followed by a helping word (some time ago).

2. When two words, *some time* can be replaced with an equivalent expression. *Sometime* cannot. 'Some time ago' can be replaced with 'a short time ago', 'a long time ago', etc.

3. When spoken, there is greater stress placed on *time* when *some time* is two words.

In practice the distinctions cause less trouble to users of English than to those who try to explain them.

some time. See SOMETIME, SOME TIME.

sort. 'Mr Hawkins said that Mr Webster was a pretty seasoned operator when it came to dealing with these sort of things' (*The Times*). Make it 'this sort of thing' or 'these sorts of things'.

spate. 'The recent spate of takeover offers has focused attention on the sector' (*Observer*). The reference here was to half a dozen takeover offers – a flurry. *Spate* should be used to describe a torrent. See also PLETHORA.

spit. See EXPECTORATE, SPIT.

split compound verbs. Some writers, apparently inspired by a misguided dread of the split infinitive (which see), are equally fastidious about not breaking up compound verbs, whatever the cost to idiom and clarity. (A compound verb is one made up of two elements, such as *has been*, *will go*, *is doing*.) The practice is particularly rife in America, where sentences like the following are more or less standard on many papers: 'It is yet to be demonstrated that a national magazine effectively can cover cable listings' (*Wall Street Journal*); 'Hitler never has been portrayed with more credibility' (*Boston Globe*); 'It always has stood as one of the last great events in amateur sports' (*Los Angeles Times*).

It cannot be stressed vigorously enough that there is no harm whatever in placing an adverb between the two elements of a compound verb. It contravenes no rule and flouts no authority. It is usually the natural place – and frequently the only place – for an adverb to go.

Those writers who so scrupulously avoid offending the integrity of a compound verb must be unaware that they disregard their self-imposed rule every time they write 'He is not going' or 'Have you been waiting long?' or 'Is it raining?' Otherwise they would almost certainly change those sentences to 'He is going not' and 'Have been waiting long you?' and 'Is raining it?' That would hardly be more illogical and contorted than 'effectively can cover' and 'always has stood'.

There are, of course, many instances in which the adverb can happily stand apart from the compound verb – 'He was working feverishly'; 'You must go directly to bed'; 'The time is passing quickly' – but forcibly evicting it for the sake of making words conform to some arbitrary pattern does a disservice to English.

split infinitives. It is probably safe to say that the number of people who would never split an infinitive is a good deal larger than the number of people who actually know what an infinitive is and does.

That may account for the number of misconceptions that litter the issue. One is the belief that the split infinitive is a grammatical error. It's not. If it is an error at all, it is a rhetorical fault – a question of style – and not a grammatical one. Another is the curiously persistent belief that the split infinitive is widely condemned. That too is untrue. No one would ever argue that a split infinitive is a good thing, but it is certainly no worse than some of the excruciating constructions foisted on us by those who regard it with an almost pathological dread. Consider these three sentences, all from *The Times* and all with a certain ring of desperation about them: 'The agreement is unlikely significantly to increase the average price'; 'It was a nasty snub for the Stock Exchange and caused it radically to rethink its ideas'; 'The education system had failed adequately to meet the needs of industry and commerce, he said'.

The problem in each instance is one of a simple conflict between the needs of the infinitive and the needs of the adverb. The natural position for the two elements of a full infinitive is together: 'He proceeded *to climb* the ladder'. With adverbs the most natural position is, very generally, just before the verb: 'He *slowly* climbed the ladder' The problem of the split infinitive occurs when the two are brought together: 'He proceeded *to slowly climb* the ladder'.

The authorities are almost unanimously agreed that there is no reason to put the needs of the infinitive above those of the adverb.

In practice the problem can usually be circumvented. Most adverbs are portable and can be moved to a position from which they can perform their function without interfering with the infinitive. In the example above, for instance, we could say: 'He proceeded to climb the ladder slowly' or 'Slowly he proceeded to climb the ladder'. But that is not to say that there is any grammatical basis for regarding the infinitive as inviolable.

When moving the adverb produces ambiguity or, to use Fowler's words, patent artificiality, the cure is at least as bad as the disease. Consider again one of the *Times* sentences: 'The education system had failed adequately to meet the needs of industry, he said'. The adverb here is clearly out of place. As written, the sentence suggests that the education system had set out to fail and had done so adequately. Partridge cites this sentence: 'Our object is to further cement trade relations'. Moving the adverb could only result in clumsiness ('further to cement') or ambiguity ('to cement further'). Bernstein cites these constructions, all crying out to be left alone: 'to more than double', 'to at least maintain', 'to all but insure'.

If you wish you may remain blindly intolerant of the split infinitive, but you should do so with the understanding that you are without the support of a single authority. Even Partridge, that most deeply conservative of scholars, is against you. He says: 'Avoid the split infinitive wherever possible; but if it is the clearest and most natural construction, use it boldly. The angels are on our side'.

spoonfuls, not spoonsful or spoons full. Bernstein cites the following: 'Now throw in two tablespoons full of chopped parsley and cook ten minutes more. The quail ought to be tender by then'. As Bernstein says, 'Never mind the quail; how are we ever going to get those tablespoons tender?'.

stalemate. 'Senators Back Rise in Proposed Oil Tax as Stalemate Ends' (*New York Times* headline). Stalemates don't end. 'Deadlock' would have been better.

stanch, staunch. 'He showed how common soldiers ... had fought their fears, staunched their wounds and met their deaths' (*Newsweek*). Although *staunch* is given as an acceptable variant by most dictionaries, *stanch* is the preferred spelling for the verb. As an adjective, *staunch* is the only spelling ('a staunch supporter').

stationary, stationery. The difference in spelling has been observed for centuries, though etymologically there isn't any basis for it. Both words come from the Latin *stationarius* and both originally meant 'standing in a fixed position'. Stationers were tradesmen, usually booksellers, who sold their wares from a fixed spot (as opposed to itinerants). Today in Britain stationery is still sold by stationers, which makes the misspelling there less excusable, if no less frequent. It applies not just to writing paper and envelopes but to all office materials. Strictly speaking, paper clips and pencils are stationery.

stationery. See STATIONARY, STATIONERY.

staunch. See STANCH, STAUNCH.

straitjacket. Often misspelled, as here: 'She was beaten, put into a home-made straightjacket and fed mustard sandwiches' (*Standard*). *Strait* means confined and restricted, as in 'straitened circumstances'. Apart from the pronunciation, it has nothing in common with 'straight'.

strata, stratum. One stratum, two strata. See DATA.

stratum. See STRATA, STRATUM.

strike action has, distressingly and perplexingly, become almost the invariable expression in Britain, as here: 'The report says 2,500 engineers and technicians are threatening strike action because of the crisis' (*Sunday Times*). Why not 'are threatening to strike'?

subjunctives. The subjunctive, one of the four moods of verbs, is falling increasingly into disuse, at least as a recognizable form. Partridge was perhaps its last defender. In *Usage and Abusage* he insisted that 'Although he die now, his name will live' was vastly superior to 'Although he dies now, his name will live'. But constructions of the first sort are almost never encountered now and no other authority argues for them. The subjunctive does survive, however, in three other types of construction. These are:

1. In certain stock phrases: 'be that as it may', 'God forbid', 'far be it from me', 'come what may', 'so be it', 'as it were' and many others. These are well established as idioms and normally cause no trouble.

2. In expressions involving suppositions or hypotheses: 'If I were you, I wouldn't go'. These are treated under IF and WILL, WOULD.

3. Following verbs of command or request. This problem scarcely exists in America, where this form of the subjunctive has always been part of the native speech, but is endlessly repeated in Britain. In the following instances the correct form is given in parentheses: 'The Senate has now rewritten the contract insisting that the Navy considers (consider) other options' (*Daily Mail*); 'Opec's monitoring committee has recommended that the cartel's output ceiling remains (remain) unchanged' (*The Times*); 'No wonder the Tory Party turned him down as a possible candidate, suggesting he went away (go away) and came back (come back) with a better public image' (*Guardian*). In each of those it might help to imagine placing a 'should' just before the problem verb (e.g., 'suggesting he should go away'). Gowers in fact suggests that such sentences would be better in British usage if 'should' were written in.

substitute can be followed only by 'for'. You substitute one thing for another. If you find yourself following the word with 'by' or 'with' or any other preposition, you should choose another word.

subsume. As Safire notes, the word has a great appeal to those who cannot resist a pretentious variation, but it is also frequently misused. It does not mean to consume or make subordinate, as is often thought. It means to be considered as part of a greater whole. *The Shorter O E D* gives this example: 'In the judgment "all horses are animals", the conception "horses" is subsumed under that of "animals"'. Does that sound like a word you really need?

successfully. 'Japanese researchers have successfully developed a semi-conductor chip made of gallium arsenide' (*Associated Press*). It was thoughtful of the writer to tell us that the researchers had not unsuccessfully developed a gallium arsenide chip, but also unnecessary. Delete *successfully*.

supersede. Probably more people visit Antarctica each year than spell *supersede* correctly. Those who habitualy make it *supercede* may take some comfort in knowing that the word caused just as much trouble to the ancient Romans, who often couldn't decide between *supersedere* and *supercedere*. *Supercede* was in early English usage an acceptable variant, but no longer.

supine. See PRONE, PROSTRATE, RECUMBENT, SUPINE.

surrounded. 'Often shrouded by fog and surrounded on three sides by surging seas, the gray stone lighthouse looms like a medieval keep' (*Time*); 'The waterworks is right in the middle of suburban Sutton and completely surrounded by houses' (*Sunday Express*). The first usage is wrong, the second superfluous. If you are not completely encircled, you are not surrounded. *Surrounded* should be changed in the first example to cut off or bordered and 'completely' should be deleted from the second.

sympathy. See EMPATHY, SYMPATHY, COMPASSION, PITY, COMMISERATION.

take place. See OCCUR, TAKE PLACE.

target. To most people there are really only two things you can do with a target: you can hit it or you can miss it. But for journalists and politicians, targets are things to be achieved, attained, exceeded, expanded, reduced, obtained, met, beaten, overtaken and metaphorically shaken to bits. As a consequence their statements are often a little absurd and more than a little ambiguous, as here: 'More welcome news came with the announcement that the public sector borrowing requirement now appears likely to undershoot its target for the full year' (*The Times*). An archer who undershoots his target will be chagrined. A politician will apparently be pleased. The reader may merely be confused.

To protest too much is quibbling – in practice, target often is the most efficient word for conveying a point concisely, even if the literal meaning is sometimes a bit strained – but it is worth seeing if 'objective' or 'plan' wouldn't work as well.

Even more worth watching are instances in which *target* gets mixed up with other metaphors. Philip Howard cites this curious headline from *The Times*: '£6m ceiling keeps rise in earnings well within Treasury target'.

tautology, redundancy, pleonasm, solecism. Although various authorities detect various shades of distinction between the first three words, those distinctions are always very slight and, on comparison, are frequently contradictory. Essentially all three mean using more words than necessary to convey an idea.

Not all repetition is bad. It may be used for effect, as in poetry, or for clarity, or as a consequence of idiom. 'OPEC countries', 'SALT talks' and 'TUC Congress' are all technically redundant because the second word is already contained in the preceding abbreviation, but only the ultra-finicky would deplore them. Similarly in 'wipe that smile off your face' the last two words are tautological – there is no other place that a smile could be – but the sentence would not stand without them.

On the whole, however, the use of more words than necessary is almost always better avoided, though it occurs among even the most careful writers, as here: 'All writers and speakers of English, including these very grammarians themselves, omit words which will never be missed' (Bergen and Cornelia Evans in *A Dictionary of Contemporary American Usage*). The use of 'these very' ahead of 'grammarians' makes 'themselves' unnecessary. Either delete 'themselves' or delete 'very'.

Finally, *solecism* describes any violation of idiom or grammar. Redundancies, tautologies and pleonasms are all solecisms.

temperature. See FEVER, TEMPERATURE.

temporary respite. 'Even Saudi Arabia's assurance that it would not cut oil prices provided no more than a temporary respite' (*Daily Telegraph*). The expression is common, but redundant. A respite can only be temporary.

terribly, awfully, horribly, etc. The tendency to use words such as these in senses contrary to their literal meanings ('That's terribly good', 'You're awfully funny') is not, as Fowler notes, confined to English. The ancient Greeks abused their word for *awfully* in much the same way. But the habit is better resisted and has no place in formal writing.

than. Three problems here:

1. 'Nearly twice as many people die under 20 in France than in Great Britain' (cited by Gowers). Make it 'as in Great Britain'.

2. 'Hardly had I landed at Liverpool than the Mikado's death recalled me to Japan' (cited by Fowler). Make it 'No sooner had I landed than' or 'Hardly had I landed when'.

3. Should you say, 'She likes tennis more than me' or 'more than I'? It depends on whether you mean that she likes tennis more than she likes me (first example) or that she likes tennis more than I do (second example). In either case, it is better to provide a second verb if there is a chance of ambiguity or a look of overfussiness, e.g., 'She likes tennis more than she likes me' and 'She likes tennis more than I do'. Fowler provides a good example of ambiguity: 'I would rather you shot the poor dog than me'.

that (as a conjunction). Whether you say 'I think you are wrong' or 'I think that you are wrong' is partly a matter of idiom but mostly a matter of preference. Some words usually require *that* (assert, contend, maintain) and some do not (say, think). On the whole it is better to dispense with *that* when it isn't necessary.

that, which. To understand the distinctions between *that* and *which* it is necessary to understand defining and non-defining clauses. Learning these distinctions is not, it must be said, anyone's idea of a good time, but it is one technical aspect of grammar that every professional user of English should understand because it is at the root of an assortment of grammatical errors.

A non-defining clause is one that can be regarded as parenthetical: 'The tree, *which had no leaves*, was a birch'. The italicized words are effectively an aside and could be deleted. The real point of the sentence is that the tree was a birch; its leaflessness is incidental. A defining clause is one that is essential to the sense of the sentence: 'The tree *that had no leaves* was a birch'. Here the leaflessness is a defining characteristic; it helps us to distinguish that tree from other trees.

In correct usage *that* is always used to indicate defining clauses and *which* to indicate non-defining ones. Defining clauses should never be set off with commas and non-defining clauses always should. On that much the authorities are agreed. Where divergence creeps in is on the question of how strictly the distinctions should be observed.

Until relatively recently they were not observed at all. In the King James Bible, for instance, we find: 'Render therefore unto Caesar the things which are Caesar's; and unto God the things that are God's'. The same quotation appears twice more in the Bible – once with *that* in both places and once with *which* in both. Today, *that* is more usual in short sentences or early on in longer ones ('The house that Jack built', 'The mouse that roared'). *Which* often appears where *that* would more strictly be correct, particularly in Britain, as here: 'It has outlined two broad strategies which it thinks could be put to the institutions' (*The Times*).

Although there is ample precedent for using *which* in defining clauses, the practice is on the whole better avoided. There are, at any rate, occasions when the choice of *which* is clearly wrong, as here: 'On a modest estimate, public authorities own 100,000 houses, which remain unoccupied for at least a year' (*Sunday Times*). What the writer meant was that of those houses that are publicly owned, at least 100,000 are left vacant for a year or more. Deleting the comma after 'houses' and changing *which* to *that* would have made this immediately clear.

Another common fault – more a discourtesy to the reader than an error – is the failure to set off non-defining clauses with commas, as here: 'Four members of one of the world's largest drugs rings (,) which smuggled heroin worth £5 million into Britain (,) were jailed yesterday' (*The Times*). That lapse is seen only rarely in America, but is rife in Britain; it occurred five times more in the same article.

Americans, on the other hand, are much more inclined to use *that* where *which* might be preferable, as here: 'Perhaps, with the help of discerning decision-makers, the verb can regain its narrow definition that gave it a reason for being' (William Safire, *On Language*). Had Safire written 'can regain *the* narrow meaning that gave it a reason for being', all would be well. But the use of 'its' gives the final clause the feel of a non-defining afterthought and the sentence might be better rendered as 'can regain its narrow definition, which gave it a reason for being'. The point is arguable.

thinking to oneself. 'Somehow he must have thought to himself that this unfamiliar line needed to be ascribed to someone rather more venerable' (*Sunday Telegraph*); '"Can it be that the Sunday Times Magazine is paying no attention to my book?" Frank Delaney was thinking to himself' (*Sunday Times*). Scrub 'to himself' both times; there is no one else to whom you can think. Similarly vacuous is 'in my mind' here: 'I could picture in my mind where the bookkeeping offices had been ...' (*Boston Globe*).

though, although. The two are interchangeable except at the end of a sentence, where only *though* is correct ('He looked tired, though') and with the expressions *as though* and *even though*, where idiom precludes *although*.

till. See UNTIL, TILL, 'TIL, 'TILL.

'til. See UNTIL, TILL, 'TIL, 'TILL.

'till. See UNTIL, TILL, 'TIL, 'TILL.

time. Often used superfluously in constructions of this sort: 'The report will be available in two weeks time' (*Guardian*). *Time* adds nothing to the sentence but length and its deletion would obviate the need for an apostrophe after 'weeks'.

tirade. See HARANGUE, TIRADE.

together with, along with. *With* in both expressions is a preposition, not a conjunction, and therefore does not govern the verb. This sentence is wrong: 'They said the man, a motor mechanic, together with a 22-year-old arrested a day earlier, were being questioned' (*The Times*). Make it 'was being questioned'.

A separate danger with such expressions is seen here: 'Barbara Tuchman, the historian, gave $20,000 to the Democrats, along with her husband, Lester' (*The New York Times*). How Lester felt about being given to the Democrats wasn't recorded.

ton, tonne. There are two kinds of tons: a long ton weighing 2,240 pounds and a short ton weighing 2,000 pounds. A tonne is a metric ton weighing 1,000 kilograms, or about 2,204 pounds.

tonne. See TON, TONNE.

tortuous, torturous. *Tortuous* means winding and circuitous ('The road wound tortuously through the mountains'). When used figuratively it usually suggests crookedness or deviousness ('a tortuous tax-avoidance scheme'). The word is thus better avoided if all you mean is complicated or convoluted. *Torturous* is the adjectival form of *torture* and describes the infliction of extreme pain.

torturous. See TORTUOUS, TORTUROUS.

total. There are three points to note here:

1. *Total* is redundant and should be deleted when what it is qualifying already contains the idea of a totality, as here: '[They] risk total annihilation at the hands of the massive Israeli forces now poised to strike at the gates of the city' (*Washington Post*).

2. The expression *a total of*, though common, is also generally superfluous: 'County officials said a total of 84 prisoners were housed in six cells ...' (*The New York Times*). Make it 'officials said 84 prisoners'. An exception is at the start of sentences when it is desirable to avoid spelling out a large number, as in 'A total of 212 sailors were aboard' instead of 'Two hundred and twelve sailors were aboard', though recasting is often better still: 'There were 212 sailors on board'.

3. 'A total of 45 weeks was spent on the study' (*The Times*) is wrong.

As with 'a number of' and 'the number of', the rule is to make it 'the total of ... was' but 'a total of ... were'.

toward, towards. The first is the preferred form in America, the second in Britain, but either is correct. *Untoward*, however, is the only accepted form in both.

towards. See TOWARD, TOWARDS.

transatlantic. 'The agreement came just in time to stop the authorities from taking away his permits to operate trans-Atlantic flights' (*Sunday Times*). Most dictionaries prefer *transatlantic*. Similarly, *transalpine*, *transarctic*, *transpacific*.

transpire. 'But Mayor Koch had a different version of what transpired [at the hotel]' (*The New York Times*). *Transpire* does not mean occur, as was intended above. Still less does it mean arrive or be received, as was intended here: 'And generally the group found it had too many stocks for the orders that transpired' (*The Times*). It means to leak out (literally in Latin 'to breathe through').

treble. See TRIPLE, TREBLE.

triple, treble. Either word can be used as a noun, verb or adjective. Except in certain musical senses, *triple* is used almost exclusively for all three in America and is becoming increasingly preponderant in Britain. According to Fowler, *treble* is more usual as a verb ('They trebled their profits') and as a noun ('I will give you treble what he offered'). As an adjective, he says, *treble* is preferable for amount and *triple* for kinds. Thus 'treble difficulty' should describe something that is three times as difficult and 'triple difficulty' should describe a difficulty made up of three things.

trivia is a plural. 'All this trivia is a nuisance' should be 'All these trivia are a nuisance'. There is no singular form (the Latin *trivium* now has only historical applications) but there are the singular words *trifle* and *triviality*. The other option is to rework *trivia* into its adjectival form: 'Such a trivial matter is a nuisance'.

true facts. 'No one in the White House seems able to explain why it took such a potentially fatal time to inform the Vice President of the true facts' (*Sunday Times*). *True facts* is always either redundant or incorrect. A fact is not a fact unless it is true.

try and is colloquial and better avoided in serious writing. 'The Monopolies Commission will look closely at retailing mergers to try and prevent any lessening of competition' (*Sunday Times*). Make it 'try to prevent'.

tumult, turmoil. Both describe confusion and agitation. The difference is that *tumult* applies only to people, but *turmoil* applies to both people and things. *Tumultuous*, however, can describe things as well as people ('tumultuous applause', 'tumultuous seas').

turbid. See TURGID, TURBID.

turgid, turbid. It is seldom possible to tell with certainty whether the writer is using *turgid* in its proper sense or is confusing it with *turbid*, but confusion would appear to be the case here: 'She insisted on reading the entire turgid work aloud, a dusk-to-dawn affair that would have tried anyone's patience' (*Sunday Times*). *Turgid* means inflated, grandiloquent, bombastic. It does not mean muddy or impenetrable, which meanings are covered by *turbid*.

turmoil. See TUMULT, TURMOIL.

turpitude. 'As far as Jimmy Carter the man, his integrity, his moral turpitude, his commitment to government, his commitment to family, it is unimpeachable' (cited by William Safire, *On Language*). The man who made that statement – he was a member of the Carter–Mondale Presidential Committee – obviously thought *turpitude* meant rectitude or integrity. In fact, it means baseness or depravity.

UCLA. 'A professor of higher education at the University College of Los Angeles has examined the careers of 200,000 students at 350 colleges' (*Sunday Times*). The error is a common one outside North America. UCLA stands for the University of California at Los Angeles.

undoubtedly. See DOUBTLESS, UNDOUBTEDLY, INDUBITABLY.

unexceptionable, unexceptional. Sometimes confused. Something that is unexceptional is ordinary, not outstanding ('an unexceptional wine'). Something that is unexceptionable is not open to objections ('In Britain, *grey* is the preferred spelling, but *gray* is unexceptionable').

unilateral, bilateral, multilateral. These words have become such a standard part of modern political jargon that many people forget they can be replaced by simpler equivalents: one-sided, two-sided and many-sided. In any case, their presence is, as often as not, unnecessary, as here: 'Bilateral trade talks are to take place next week between Britain and Japan' (*The Times*). Trade talks between Britain and Japan could hardly be other than two-sided. Delete *bilateral*.

uninterested. See DISINTERESTED, UNINTERESTED.

unique means the only one of its kind. It is incomparable. One thing cannot be more unique than another, as was thought here: 'Lafeyette's most unique restaurant is now even more unique' (cited by Wood).

unknown is often used imprecisely, as here: 'A hitherto unknown company called Ashdown Oil has emerged as a bidder for the Wytch Farm oil interests' (*The Times*). A company must be known to someone, if only its directors. It would be better to call it a little-known company.

unless and until. One or the other, please.

unlike. When *unlike* is used as a preposition, it should govern a noun or pronoun or a noun equivalent (e.g., a gerund). 'But unlike at previous sessions of the conference ...' (*The New York Times*) needs to be 'But unlike previous sessions' or 'As was not the case at previous sessions'.

Unlike must also contrast things that are comparable, which was not done here: 'Unlike the proposal by Rep. Albert Gore, outlined in this space yesterday, the President is not putting forth a blueprint for a final treaty' (*Chicago Tribune*). As written, the sentence is telling us that a proposal is unlike the President – which should come as a surprise to no one. It should be: 'Unlike the proposal by Rep. Albert Gore, the President's plan does not put forth a blueprint' or words to that effect.

unpractical. See IMPRACTICAL, IMPRACTICABLE, UNPRACTICAL.

until, till, 'til, 'till. The first two are legitimate and interchangeable. The second two are illiterate.

up. When used as a phrasal verb (which see), *up* is often just a hitch-hiker, joining sentences only for the ride. Sometimes idiom dictates that we include it: we look up a word in a book, we dig up odd facts, we move up in our careers. But often it is needlessly attached to words, as here: 'Plans to tighten up the rules for charging overseas visitors for use of the National Health Service were announced yesterday' (*The Times*); 'Another time, another tiger ate up 27 of Henning's 30 prop animals' (*Washington Post*); 'This could force the banks to lift up their interest rates' (*Financial Times*). *Buoy up, loosen up, ring up, phone up, climb up* and countless others are all generally unnecessary and ought to be avoided. Occasionally in its eagerness *up* moves to the front of words: 'With the continued upsurge in sales of domestic appliances ...' (*The Times*). Although upsurge is a recognized word, it seldom means more than surge.

upon. See ON, UPON.

usage. See USE, USAGE.

use, usage. *Usage* describes that which is habitual and customary. But *use*, in addition to its other meanings, can also mean that. In practice, *usage* is frowned on by grammarians when it is employed by anyone other than themselves and normally it appears only in the context of languages ('modern English usage').

usual. A common oversight in newspapers – no doubt attributable to haste – is telling readers twice in one sentence that a thing is customary. Both of the following are from *The New York Times*: 'The usual procedure normally involved getting eyewitness reports of one or more acts of heroism'; 'Customarily, such freezes are usually imposed at the end of a fiscal year'. Delete something. See also HABITS.

utilize. In its strictest sense, *utilize* means to make the best use of something that wasn't intended for the job ('He utilized a coat hanger to repair his car'). It can be extended to mean making the most practical possible use of something ('Although the hills were steep, the rice farmers utilized every square inch of the land'). But in all other senses, 'use' is better.

various different is inescapably redundant.

venal, venial. *Venial*, from the Latin *venialis* ('forgivable'), means excusable. A venial sin is a minor one. *Venal* means corruptible. It comes from the Latin *venalis* ('for sale') and describes someone who is capable of being bought.

venerate, worship. Although in figurative senses the words are interchangeable, in religious contexts *worship* should apply only to God. Roman Catholics, for instance, worship God but venerate saints.

venial. See VENAL, VENIAL.

verbal. See ORAL, VERBAL.

very should be made to pay its way in sentences. All too often it is used where it adds nothing to the sense ('It was a very tragic death'), or is inserted in a futile effort to prop up a weak word that would be better replaced by something more descriptive ('The play was very good').

via, meaning 'by way of', indicates the direction of a journey ('A flight from London to Los Angeles via Boston') and not the means by which the journey is achieved. It is used incorrectly here: 'Out at the end of the wharf a man sold tickets [for] "excursion" trips via a speed boat' (cited by Partridge).

viable. 'Such a system would mark a breakthrough in efforts to come up with a commercially viable replacement for internal-combustion vehicles' (*Newsweek*); 'I believe there is a viable market for the Samba Cabriolet in Britain' (*Mail on Sunday*). *Viable* does not mean feasible or workable. It means capable of independent existence and its use really ought to be confined to that meaning. Even when it is correctly used, it tends to make the sentence read like a government document, as here: 'Doing nothing about the latter threatens the viability of the lakes and woodlands of the northeastern states' (*Chicago Tribune*). Deleting 'the viability of' would shorten the sentence without altering its sense.

virtually, practically. *Practically* means in practice or to all practical purposes. *Virtually* means almost or in effect. In most instances the words are practically/virtually indistinguishable. But there is a slight difference. *Practically* should not be used when you mean almost. As Bernstein notes, to say that you are practically out of coffee when there is enough left for a couple of cups is a bit loose because as a practical matter you are not out of coffee. That, it may be argued, is splitting hairs. But certainly to be avoided are sentences such as 'I practically won the race' when you finished second.

vocal cords have nothing to do with chords of music, as many writers seem to think: 'Understudy Nancy Ringham will play opposite Rex Harrison because Miss Kennedy has problems with her vocal chords' (*Standard*). Make it 'cords'.

vortexes, vortices. For the plural of *vortex*, either is correct. *The Concise Oxford* gives *vortices* first; *The American Heritage* gives *vortexes* first.

vortices. See VORTEXES, VORTICES.

◉ **W** ◉

warn. 'British Rail warned that the snow was bound to have a serious effect on its service today' (*Daily Telegraph*). Most British dictionaries continue not to recognize *warn* used intransitively, as it has been above. Accordingly, *warn* needs an expressed personal object – i.e., the sentence must state who or what is being warned. Thus it should be: 'British Rail warned passengers that ...'. In the United States the word may be used with or without an object.

The rule is, I think, more than a little fussy, especially when, as in the example above, a warning is general. If we are to have an expressed personal object for the sake of form, we might equally insist on the inclusion of all the objects for the sake of accuracy. Thus: 'British Rail warned passengers, freight users, people planning to meet passengers, British Rail staff, the Government, the Post Office, the police and ferry operators that snow was bound to have a serious effect on its service today'.

The weight of usage is clearly on the side of accepting the intransitive and I can find no usage authority who argues against it. But if you use it in Britain, you do so at the peril of being called incorrect.

weather conditions. 'Freezing weather conditions will continue for the rest of the week' (*The Times*). Delete *conditions*. Similarly tiresome is the American weather forecasters' fondness for 'activity', as in 'thunderstorm activity over the plains states'.

whence. 'And man will return to the state of hydrogen from whence he came' (*Sunday Telegraph*). Although there is ample precedent for the expression *from whence* – the King James Bible has the sentence 'I will lift up my eyes unto the hills from whence cometh my help' – it is redundant. *Whence* means from where. It is enough to say 'to the state of hydrogen whence he came'.

whether or not. The second two words should be dropped when *whether* is equivalent to 'if', as here: 'It is not yet known whether or not persons who become reinfected can spread the virus to other susceptible individuals' (*The New York Times*). *Or not* adds nothing there and

151

should be deleted. *Or not* is necessary, however, when what is being stressed is an alternative: 'I intend to come whether or not you like it'.

which. The belief that *which* may refer only to the preceding word and not to the whole of a preceding statement is without foundation except where there is a chance of ambiguity. The ridiculousness of the rule – and the impossibility of enforcing it consistently – is illustrated by an anecdote in the *New Yorker* cited by Gowers. A class in Philadelphia had written to a local paper's resident usage expert asking him what was wrong with the sentence 'He wrecked the car, which was due to his carelessness'. Notice how the authority hoists himself with the last three words of his reply: 'The fault lies in using *which* to refer to the statement "He wrecked the car". When *which* follows a noun, it refers to that noun as its antecedent. Therefore in the foregoing sentence it is stated that the car was due to his carelessness, which is nonsense'. See also THAT, WHICH.

who, whom. Shakespeare, Addison, Ben Jonson, Dickens, Churchill, the translators of the King James Bible and I, among many others, have all in our time been utterly flummoxed by the distinction between the relative pronouns *who* and *whom*.

The rule can be stated simply. *Whom* is used when it is the object of a preposition ('To whom it may concern') or verb ('The man whom we saw last night') or the subject of a complementary infinitive ('The person whom we took to be your father'). *Who* is used on all other occasions.

Consider now three extracts in which the wrong choice has been made: 'Mrs Hinckley said that her son had been upset by the murder of Mr Lennon, who he idolized' (*The New York Times*); 'Colombo, whom law enforcement officials have said is the head of a Mafia family in Brooklyn ...' (*The New York Times*); 'Heart-breaking decision – who to save' (*Times* headline). We can check the correctness of such sentences by imagining them as he/him constructions. For instance, would you say 'Hinckley idolized he' or 'idolized him'? Would law enforcement officers say that 'he is the head of a Mafia family' or 'him is the head'? And is it a heart-breaking decision over whether to save he or to save him? When the answer is he, use *who*; when it is him, use *whom*.

Simple, isn't it? Well, not quite. When the relative pronoun follows a preposition in a relative clause, that simple test falls to pieces. Consider this sentence from *Fortune* magazine: 'They rent it to whomever needs it'. Since we know that you say 'for whom the bell tolls' and 'to whom it may concern', it should follow that we would say 'to whomever needs it'. If we test that conclusion by imagining the sentence as a he/him construction – would they 'rent it to he' or 'rent it to him'? – we are bound to plump for *whom*. But we would be wrong. The difficulty there is that the relative pronoun is the subject of the verb 'needs' and not the object of the preposition 'to'. The sentence in effect is saying: 'They rent it to any person *who* needs it'.

Similarly, *whomever* would be wrong in these two sentences: 'We must offer it to whoever applies first'; 'Give it to whoever wants it'. Again, in effect they are saying: 'We must offer it to the person *who* applies first' and 'Give it to the person *who* wants it'. Such constructions usually involve a choice between *whoever* and *whomever* (as opposed to a simple *who* and *whom*), which should always alert you to proceed with caution. But they need not. An exception – and a rather tricky one – is seen here: 'The disputants differed diametrically as to who they thought might turn out to be the violator' (cited by Bernstein). The sentence is saying: 'The disputants differed diametrically as to the identity of the person *who* they thought might turn out to be the violator'.

By performing a little verbal gymnastics it is usually possible to decide with some confidence which case to use. But is it worth the bother? Is it reasonable that we should be required to perform an elaborate grammatical analysis to write our own language? Bernstein, in his later years, thought not. In 1975, he wrote to twenty-five authorities on usage asking if they thought there was any real point in preserving *whom* except when it is directly governed by a preposition (as in 'to whom it may concern'). Six voted to preserve *whom*, four were undecided and fifteen – among them Eric Partridge, Mario Pei, S. I. Hayakawa, William Morris and Bergen Evans – thought it should be abandoned.

English has been shedding its pronoun declensions for hundreds of years; today *who* is the only relative pronoun that is declinable. Preserving the distinction between *who* and *whom* does nothing to promote clarity or reduce ambiguity. It has become merely a source of frequent errors and perpetual uncertainty. Authorities have been tossing stones at *whom* for at least 200 years – Noah Webster was one of the first to call it needless – but the word refuses to go away.

A century from now it may be a relic. But for the moment you ignore it at the risk of being thought ignorant.

For a discussion of *who* in defining and non-defining clauses, see WHOSE.

whom. See WHO, WHOM.

whose. Two small problems here. One is the persistent belief that *whose* can apply only to people. The authorities are unanimous that there is nothing wrong with saying, 'The book, a picaresque novel whose central characters are . . .' rather than the clumsier 'a picaresque novel the central characters of which . . .'.

The second problem arises from a failure to discriminate between defining and non-defining clauses (discussed under THAT, WHICH). Consider: 'Many parents, whose children ride motorbikes, live in constant fear of an accident' (*Observer*). The writer has made the subordinate clause parenthetical. In effect he is saying: 'Many parents (whose children, by the way, ride motorbikes) live in constant fear of an accident'. He meant, of course, that the parents live in fear *because* their children ride motorbikes. The clause is defining; the commas should be removed. Gowers cites this example from a wartime training manual: 'Pilots, whose minds are dull, do not usually live long'. Removing the commas would convert an insult into sound advice.

The same problem often happens with *who*, as in this sentence from the stylebook of *The Times*: '*Normalcy* should be left to the Americans who coined it'. Had the writer meant that 'normalcy' should be left only to those Americans who participated in its coining, the lack of a comma would be correct. But we can assume he meant that it should be left to all Americans, who as a nation (and as an incidental matter) coined it. A comma is therefore required. In fact, however, Americans did not coin the word. It is several hundred years older than the United States and belongs to the English, who coined it. See NORMALCY.

widow, when combined with 'the late', is redundant, as here: 'Mrs Sadat, the widow of the late Egyptian President . . .' (*Guardian*). Make it either 'wife of the late Egyptian President' or 'widow of the Egyptian President'.

will, would. 'The plan would be phased in over 10 years and will involve extra national insurance contributions . . .' (*The Times*). The problem here is an inconsistency between what grammarians call the protasis (the condition) and the apodosis (the consequence). The sentence has begun in the subjunctive (*would*) and switched abruptly to the indicative (*will*). The same error occurs here: 'The rector, Chad Varah, has promised that work on the church will start in the New Year and would be completed within about three years' (*Standard*). In both sentences it should be either *will* both times or *would* both times.

This is not simply a matter of grammatical orderliness; it is a question of clarity – of telling the difference between what will happen and what may happen. Compare these two sentences: 'The plan will cost £400 million'; 'The plan would cost £400 million'. The first expresses a certainty. The plan either has been adopted or is certain to be adopted. The second is clearly suppositional. It is saying only that if the plan were adopted it would cost £400 million.

A common failing of British journalism is to present the suppositional as if it were a certainty. An article in the *Guardian* about union proposals urging the Prime Minister to spend more on job creation schemes went on to say: 'The proposals will create up to 20,000 new jobs ... will be phased in over three years ... will cost up to £8 million' and so on. In each instance the sentence should be qualified: 'The proposals *would* create up to 20,000 jobs' or 'If they are adopted, the proposals *will* cost up to £8 million'.

For the differences between *will* and *shall*, see SHALL, WILL.

worship. See VENERATE, WORSHIP.

worst comes to worst is the correct expression, not *worse comes to worst* or *worse comes to worse*, however much more logical they may be.

would. See WILL, WOULD.

wrack. See RACK, WRACK.

wrapped. See RAPT, WRAPPED.

◉ Y ◉

ye, as in Ye Old Antique Shoppe, is no more pronounced 'yee' than 'lb' is pronounced 'ulb' or 'cwt' is pronounced 'kwut'. It is an abbreviation of *the*, not another word for it. It started as an incorrect transcription of the runic letter called thorn (þ) and was perpetuated by early printers when they needed to abbreviate *the* to justify a line of type. A similar pronunciation error is often made with 'olde worlde'. Those who say 'oldie worldie' should be corrected at once and instructed never to say it again.

yes, no. Writers are often at a loss when deciding what to do with a *yes* or *no* in constructions such as the following: 'Will this really be the last of Clouseau? Blake Edwards says No' (*Sunday Express*). There are two possibilities, neither of which the writer has used. You may make it 'Blake Edwards says no' or you may make it 'Blake Edwards says, "No"'. Capitalizing the word without providing the punctuation is a pointless compromise and should satisfy no one.

yesterday. Anyone not familiar with newspaper offices could be forgiven for assuming that journalists must talk something like this: 'I last night went to bed early because I this morning had to catch an early flight'. That, at any rate, is how many of them write. Consider: 'Their decision was yesterday being heralded as a powerful warning...' (*The Times*); 'Police were last night hunting for ...' (*Daily Mail*); 'The two sides were today to consider ...' (*Guardian*). Although in newspapers some care must be taken not to place the time element in a position where it might produce ambiguity, a more natural arrangement can almost always be found: 'was being heralded yesterday'; 'were hunting last night for'; 'were to consider today'.

Yiddish, See HEBREW, YIDDISH.

◉ Z ◉

zoom. Strictly speaking, the word should describe only a steep *upward* movement. Almost every authority stresses that point, though how much it is inspired by a desire for precision and how much by the need to find something – anything – to discuss under the letter 'Z' is never easy to say. No one, I think, would argue that zoom lenses should be used only for taking pictures of the sky, nor should the word be considered objectionable when applied to lateral movements ('The cars zoomed around the track'). But for describing downward movements ('The planes zoomed down on the city to drop their bombs') it is better avoided, especially as 'swoop' is available.

Appendix: Punctuation

The uses of punctuation marks, or stops, are so numerous and the abuses so varied that the following is offered only as a very general guide to the most common errors. For those who wish to dig more deeply, I recommend the excellent *Mind the Stop* by G. V. Carey, published by Penguin.

apostrophe. The principal functions of the apostrophe are to indicate omitted letters (*don't, can't, wouldn't*) and to show the possessive (strictly, the genitive) case (*John's book, the bank's money, the people's choice*).

In its more general uses the apostrophe normally causes little trouble to educated writers (though the *Observer* still occasionally devotes a section to 'Childrens Books'). But among advertisers it is endlessly, maddeningly, distressingly neglected. I have before me a holiday brochure offering 'This years holidays at last years prices'. 'Todays Tesco' offers its customers 'mens clothes', 'womens clothes' and 'childrens clothes'. In one thinnish Sunday supplement, nine advertisers clocked up fourteen such errors between them. The mistake is inexcusable and those who make it are linguistic Neanderthals.

Two other types of error occur with some frequency and are worth noting. They involve:

1. *Multiple possessives.* This problem can be seen here: 'This is a sequel to Jeremy Paul's and Alan Gibson's play ...' (*The Times*). The question is whether both of the apostrophes are necessary, and the answer in this instance is no. Because the reference is to a single play written jointly, only the second-named man needs to be in the possessive. Thus it should be: 'Jeremy Paul and Alan Gibson's play'. If the reference were to two or more plays written separately, both names would have to carry apostrophes. The rule is that when possession is held in common, only the nearer antecedent should be possessive; when possession is separate, each antecedent must be in the possessive.

2. *Plural units of measure.* Many writers who would never think of omitting the apostrophes in 'a fair day's pay for a fair day's work' often do exactly that when the unit of measure is increased. Consider:

'Laker gets further 30 days credit' (*Times* headline); 'Mr Taranto, who had 30 years service with the company . . .' (*The New York Times*). Both 'days' and 'years' should carry an apostrophe. Alternatively we could insert an 'of' after the time elements ('30 days of credit', '19 years of service'). One or the other is necessary.

The problem is often aggravated by the inclusion of excess verbiage, as in each of these examples: 'The scheme could well be appropriate in 25 years time, he said' (*The Times*); 'Many diplomats are anxious to settle the job by the end of the session in two weeks time' (*Observer*); 'The Government is prepared to part with several hundred acres worth of property' (*Time*). Each requires an apostrophe. But that need could be obviated by excluding the superfluous wordage. What is 'in 25 years' time' if not 'in 25 years'? What does 'several hundred acres' worth of property' say that 'several hundred acres' does not?

colon. The colon marks a formal introduction or indicates the start of a series. A colon should not separate a verb from its object in simple enumerations. Thus it would be wrong to say: 'The four states bordering Texas are: New Mexico, Arkansas, Oklahoma and Louisiana'. The colon should be removed. But it would be correct to say: 'Texas is bordered by four states: New Mexico, Arkansas, Oklahoma and Louisiana'.

comma. The trend these days is to use the comma as sparingly as form and clarity allow. But there are certain instances in which it should appear but all too often does not. Equally, it has a tendency to crop up with alarming regularity in places where it has no business. It is, in short, the most abused of punctuation marks and one of the worst offenders of any kind in the English language. Essentially there are three situations where the comma's use is compulsory and a fourth where it is recommended.

1. *When the information provided is clearly parenthetical.* Consider these two sentences, both of which are correctly punctuated: 'Mr Lawson, the Energy Secretary, was unavailable for comment'; 'The ambassador, who arrived in Britain two days ago, yesterday met with the Prime Minister'. In both sentences, the information between the commas is incidental to the main thought. You could remove it and the sentence would still make sense. In the following examples, the writer has failed to set off the parenthetical information. I have provided stroke marks (the proper name, incidentally, is virgules) to show

where the commas should have gone: 'British cars/says a survey/are more reliable than their foreign counterparts' (leader in the *Standard*); 'The new AT&T Tower on Madison Avenue/the first of a new breed/ will be ready by the end of 1982' (*Sunday Times*); 'Operating mainly from the presidential palace at Baabda/southeast of Beirut, Habib negotiated over a 65-day period' (*Time*); 'Mary Chatillon, director of the Massachusetts General Hospital's Reading Language Disorder Unit/maintains: "It would simply appear to be ..."' (*Time*). It should perhaps be noted that failure to put in a comma is particularly common after a parenthesis, as here: 'Mr James Grant, executive director of the United Nations Children's Fund (UNICEF)/says ...' (*The Times*).

Occasionally the writer recognizes that the sentence contains a parenthetical thought, but fails to discern just how much of the information is incidental, as here: 'At nine she won a scholarship to Millfield, the private school, for bright children of the rich' (*Standard*). If we removed what has been presented as parenthetical, the sentence would say: 'At nine she won a scholarship to Millfield for bright children'. There should be no comma after 'school' because the whole of the last statement is parenthetical.

A rarer error is seen here: 'But its big worry is the growing evidence that such ostentatious cars, the cheapest costs £55,240, are becoming socially unacceptable' (*The Times*). When the incidental information could stand alone as a sentence, it needs to be set off with stronger punctuation – either dashes or parentheses.

2. *When the information is non-defining.* The problem here – which is really much the same as that discussed in the previous three paragraphs – is illustrated by this incorrectly punctuated sentence from the *Daily Mail*: 'Cable TV would be socially divisive, the chairman of the BBC George Howard claimed last night'. The writer has failed to understand the distinction between (1) 'BBC chairman George Howard claimed last night' and (2) 'The chairman of the BBC, George Howard, claimed last night'. In (1), the name George Howard is essential to the sense of the sentence; it defines it. If we removed it, the sentence would say: 'BBC chairman claimed last night'. In (2), however, the name is non-defining. In effect it is parenthetical. We could remove it without altering the sense of the sentence: 'The chairman of the BBC claimed last night'. When a name or title can be removed, it should be set off with commas. When it cannot be removed, the use of commas is wrong.

Two hypothetical examples may help to clarify the distinction. Both are correctly punctuated. 'John Fowles's novel *The Collector* was a best-seller'; 'John Fowles's first novel, *The Collector*, was a best-seller'. In the first example the name of the novel is defining because *The Collector* is only one of several novels by Fowles. In the second example it is non-defining because only one novel can be the author's first one. We could delete *The Collector* from the second example without spoiling the sense of the sentence, but not from the first.

When something is the only one of its kind, it should be set off with commas; when it is only one of several, the use of commas is wrong. Thus these two sentences, both from *The Times*, are incorrect: 'When the well-known British firm, Imperial Metal Industries, developed two new types of superconducting wires ...'; 'The writer in the American magazine, *Horizon*, was aware of this pretentiousness ...'. The first example would be correct only if Imperial Metal Industries were the only well-known British firm, and the second would be correct only if *Horizon* were America's only magazine. The same error in reverse occurs here: 'Julie Christie knows that in the week her new film *The Return of the Soldier* has opened ...' (*Sunday Times*). Since *The Return of the Soldier* was Julie Christie's only new film of the week, it should have been set off with commas.

The error frequently occurs when a marriage partner is named: 'Mrs Thatcher and her husband Denis left London yesterday' (*Observer*). Since Mrs Thatcher has only one husband, it should be 'and her husband, Denis, left London yesterday'.

3. *With forms of address*. When addressing people, commas are obligatory around the names or titles of those addressed. 'Hit him Jim, hit him' (*Sunday Times*) should be 'Hit him, Jim, hit him'. The BBC television series *Yes Minister* should be *Yes, Minister*. The film *I'm All Right Jack* should have been *I'm All Right, Jack*. The lack of a comma or commas is always sloppy and occasionally ambiguous. In 1981, for instance, the *Sunday Express* illustrated a novel serialization with the heading 'I'm choking Mr Herriot' when what it meant was 'I'm choking, Mr Herriot' – quite another matter.

4. *With interpolated words or phrases*. Words such as *moreover*, *meanwhile* and *nevertheless* and phrases such as *for instance* and *for example* traditionally have taken commas, but the practice has become increasingly discretionary over the years. In Britain they have been more freely abandoned than in America; Fowler, for instance, seldom

uses them. I would recommend using them when they suggest a pause or when ambiguity might result. This is especially true of *however*. Consider these two sentences: 'However hard he tried, he failed'; 'However, he tried hard, but failed'. To keep from confusing the reader, if only momentarily, it is a good idea to set off *however* with commas when it is used as an interpolation. Much the same could be said of *say*: 'She should choose a British Government stock with (,) say (,) five years to run' (*Daily Mail*).

dash. Dashes should be used in pairs to enclose parenthetical matter or singly to indicate a sharp break in a sentence ('I can't see a damn thing in here – ouch!') or to place emphasis on a point ('There are only two things we can count on – death and taxes'). Dashes are most effective when used sparingly and there should never be more than one pair in a single sentence. Fowler insists that when dashes are used in pairs, any punctuation interrupted by the first dash should be picked up after the second (e.g., 'If this is true – and no one can be sure that it is –, we should do something'). But on this, as with so much else to do with punctuation, Fowler is at odds with almost everyone else. There are two common errors with dashes:

1. Failing to mark the end of a parenthetical comment with a second dash: 'The group – it is the largest in its sector, with subsidiaries or associates in 11 countries, says trading has improved in the current year' (*The Times*). Make it 'countries – says'.

2. Allowing a word or phrase from the main part of the sentence to become locked within the parenthetical area, as here: 'There is another institution which appears to have an even more – shall we say, relaxed – attitude to security' (*The Times*). Removing the words between the dashes would give us an institution with 'an even more attitude'. *Relaxed* belongs to the sentence proper and needs to be put outside the dashes: 'There is another institution which appears to have an even more – shall we say? – relaxed attitude to security'. (See also PARENTHESES.)

ellipsis. An ellipsis (sometimes called an ellipse) is used to indicate that material has been omitted. It consists of three full stops (...) and not, as some writers think, a random scattering of them. When an ellipsis occurs at the end of a sentence, a fourth full stop is normally added.

exclamation marks are used to show strong emotion ('Get out!') or urgency ('Help me!'). They should almost never be used for giving emphasis to a simple statement of fact: 'It was bound to happen sometime! A bull got into a china shop here' (cited by Bernstein).

full stop (US, period). There are two common errors associated with the full stop, both of which arise from its absence. The first is the run-on sentence (that is, the linking of two complete thoughts by a comma). It is never possible to say when a run-on sentence is attributable to ignorance on the part of the writer or to whimsy on the part of the typesetter, but the error occurs frequently enough that ignorance must play a part. In each of the following I have indicated with a stroke where one sentence should end and the next should begin: 'Although GEC handled the initial contract, much of the equipment is American,/the computers and laser printers come from Hewlett Packard' (*Guardian*); 'Confidence is growing that Opec will resolve its crisis,/however the Treasury is drawing up contingency plans' (*The Times*); 'Funds received in this way go towards the cost of electricity and water supply,/industries, shops and communes pay higher rates' (*The Times*).

The second lapse arises when a writer tries to say too much in a single sentence, as here: 'The measures would include plans to boost investment for self-financing in industry, coupled with schemes to promote investment and saving, alleviate youth unemployment, fight inflation and lower budget deficits, as well as a new look at the controversial issue of reducing working hours' (*The Times*). If the writer has not lost his readers, he has certainly lost himself. The last lumbering flourish ('as well as a new look . . .') is grammatically unconnected to what has gone before; it just hangs there. The sentence is crying out for a full stop – almost anywhere would do – to give the reader a chance to absorb the wealth of information being provided.

Here is another in which the writer tells us everything but his phone number: 'But after they had rejected once more the umpires' proposals of $5,000 a man for the playoffs and $10,000 for the World Series on a three-year contract and the umpires had turned down a proposal of $3,000 for the playoffs and $7,000 for the World Series on a one-year contract, baseball leaders said the playoffs would begin today and they had umpires to man the games' (*The New York Times*).

There is no quota on full stops. When an idea is complicated, break it up and present it in digestible chunks. One idea to a sentence is still the best advice that anyone has ever given on writing.

hyphen. Almost nothing can be said with finality about the hyphen. As Fowler says, 'its infinite variety defies description'. Even the word for using a hyphen is contentious: some authorities hyphenate words, but others hyphen them. The principal function of the hyphen is to reduce the chances of ambiguity. Consider, for instance, the distinction between 'the 20-odd members of his Cabinet' and 'the 20 odd members of his Cabinet'. It is sometimes used to indicate pronunciation (de-ice), but not always (coalesce, reissue). Composite adjectives used before a noun are usually given hyphens (a six-foot-high wall, a four-inch rainfall), but again not always. Fowler cites 'a balance-of-payments deficit' and Gowers 'a first-class ticket', but in expressions such as these, where the words are frequently linked, the hyphens are no more necessary than they would be in 'a trade-union conference' or 'a Post-Office strike'. When the phrases are used adverbially, the use of hyphens is wrong, as here: 'Mr Conran, who will be 50-years-old next month ...' (*Sunday Times*). Mr Conran will be 50 years old next month; he will then be a 50-year-old man.

In general, hyphens should be dispensed with when they are not necessary. One place where they are not required by sense but frequently occur anyway is with '-ly' adverbs, as in 'newly-elected' or 'widely-held'. Almost every authority suggests that they should be deleted in such constructions.

parentheses. Parenthetical matter can be thought of as any information so incidental to the main thought that it needs to be separated from the sentence that contains it. It can be set off with dashes, brackets (usually reserved for explanatory insertions in quotations), commas or, of course, parentheses. It is, in short, an insertion and has no grammatical effect on the sentence in which it appears. It is rather as if the sentence does not even know it is there. Thus this statement from *The Times* is incorrect: 'But that is not how Mrs Graham (and her father before her) have made a success of the *Washington Post*'. The verb should be 'has'.

But while the parenthetical expression has no grammatical effect on the sentence in which it appears, the sentence does influence the parenthesis. Consider this extract from the *Los Angeles Times* (which, although it uses dashes, could equally have employed parentheses): 'One reason for the dearth of Japanese-American politicians is that no Japanese immigrants were allowed to become citizens – and thus could not vote – until 1952'. As written the sentence is telling us that 'no Japanese citizens could not vote'. Delete 'could not'.

When a parenthetical comment is part of a larger sentence, the full stop should appear after the second parenthesis (as here). (But when the entire sentence is parenthetical, as here, the full stop should appear inside the final parenthesis.)

question mark. The question mark comes at the end of a question. That sounds simple enough, doesn't it? But it's astonishing how frequently writers fail to include it. Two random examples: '"Why travel all the way there when you could watch the whole thing at home," he asked' (*The Times*); 'The inspector got up to go and stood on Mr Ellis's cat, killing it. "What else do you expect from these people," said the artist' (*Standard*).

Occasionally question marks are included when they are not called for, as in this sentence by Trollope, cited by Fowler: 'But let me ask of her enemies whether it is not as good a method as any other known to be extant?' The problem here is a failure to distinguish between a direct question and an indirect one. Direct questions always take question marks: 'Who is going with you?'. Indirect questions never do: 'I would like to know who is going with you'.

When direct questions take on the tone of a command, the use of a question mark becomes more discretionary. 'Will everyone please assemble in my office at four o'clock?' is strictly correct, but not all authorities insist on the question mark there.

A less frequent problem arises when a direct question appears outside a direct quotation. Fieldhouse, in *Everyman's Good English Guide*, suggests that the following punctuation is correct: 'Why does this happen to us, we wonder?' The Fowler brothers, however, call this an amusing blunder; certainly it is extremely irregular. The more usual course is to attach the question mark directly to the question. Thus: 'Why does this happen to us? we wonder'. But such constructions are clumsy and are almost always improved by being turned into indirect questions: 'We wonder why this happens to us'.

quotation marks (inverted commas). An issue that arises frequently in Britain, but almost never in America, is whether to put full stops and other punctuation inside or outside quotation marks when they appear together. The practice that prevails almost exclusively in America and is increasingly common in Britain is to put the punctuation inside the quotes. Thus: 'He said: "I will not go."' But some publishers prefer the punctuation to fall outside except when it is part of the quotation. Thus the example above would be: 'He said: "I will not go".'

Both systems are marked by inconsistencies – even Americans are forced to put the punctuation outside the quotes in such sentences as 'Which of you said, "Look out"?' – and there is not much to choose between them on grounds of logic. Similarly, the question of whether to use single quotes (') or double quotes (") is entirely a matter of preference except when it is dictated by house-style.

When quotation marks are used to set off a complete statement, the first word of the quotation should be capitalized ('He said, "Victory is ours"') except when the quotation is preceded by 'that' ('He said that "victory is ours"'). Fowler believed that no punctuation was necessary to set off attributive quotations; he would, for instance, delete the commas from the following: 'Tomorrow', he said, 'is a new day'. His argument was that commas are not needed to mark the interruption or introduction of a quotation because the quotation marks already do that. Logically he is correct. But with equal logic we could argue that question marks should be dispensed with on the grounds that the context almost always makes it clear that a question is being asked. The commas are required not by logic but by convention.

semicolon. The semicolon is heavier than the comma but lighter than the full stop. Its principal function is to divide contact clauses – that is, two ideas that are linked by sense but that lack a conjunction. For instance: 'You take the high road; I'll take the low road'. Equally that could be made into two complete sentences or, by introducing a conjunction, into one ('You take the high road and I'll take the low road'). The semicolon is also sometimes used to separate long coordinate clauses. In this role it was formerly used much more extensively than it is today – Fowler, for instance, would often string together a whole series of semicolons. Today its use is almost entirely discretionary. Many good writers scarcely use the semicolon at all.

Bibliography

Throughout the text I have in general referred to the following books by the surname of the author, ignoring the contributions of those who revised the originals. Thus although Sir Ernest Gowers substantially revised *A Dictionary of Modern English Usage* in 1965, that book is referred to throughout the text as 'Fowler'. References to 'Gowers' are meant to suggest Gowers's own book, *The Complete Plain Words*.

Aitchison, Jean, *Language Change: Progress or Decay?*, Fontana, London, 1981.

American Heritage Dictionary, American Heritage Publishing Company, New York, 1969.

Bernstein, Theodore M., *The Careful Writer*, Atheneum, New York, 1967.
   Dos, Don'ts and Maybes of English Usage, Times Books, New York, 1977.

Carey, G. V., *Mind the Stop*, Penguin, Harmondsworth, 1971.

Collins Dictionary of the English Language, Collins, London, 1979.

Concise Oxford Dictionary of Current English, Oxford University Press, Oxford, 1982.

Evans, Bergen and Cornelia, *A Dictionary of Contemporary American Usage*, Random House, New York, 1957.

Fieldhouse, Harry, *Everyman's Good English Guide*, J. M. Dent & Sons, London, 1982.

Fowler, E. G. and H. W., *The King's English*, third edition, Oxford University Press, London, 1970.

Fowler, H. W., *A Dictionary of Modern English Usage*, second edition (revised by Sir Ernest Gowers), Oxford University Press, Oxford, 1980.

Gowers, Sir Ernest, *The Complete Plain Words*, second edition (revised by Sir Bruce Fraser), Penguin, Harmondsworth, 1980.

Howard, Philip, *New Words for Old*, Unwin, London, 1980.
   Weasel Words, Hamish Hamilton, London, 1978.
   Words Fail Me, Hamish Hamilton, London, 1980.

Hudson, Kenneth, *The Dictionary of Diseased English*, Papermac, London, 1980.

Jordan, Lewis (ed.), *The New York Times Manual of Style and Usage*, Times Books, New York, 1976.

Michaels, Leonard, and Ricks, Christopher (ed.), *The State of the Language*, University of California Press, Berkeley, 1980.

Morris, William and Mary, *Harper Dictionary of Contemporary Usage*, Harper & Row, New York, 1975.

Newman, Edwin, *Strictly Speaking*, Warner Books, New York, 1975.
  A Civil Tongue, Warner Books, New York, 1976.
Onions, C. T., *Modern English Syntax*, seventh edition (prepared by B. D. H.
  Miller), Routledge and Kegan Paul, London, 1971.
Oxford Dictionary for Writers and Editors, Oxford University Press, Oxford,
  1981.
Oxford Dictionary òf English Etymology, Oxford University Press, Oxford,
  1982.
Palmer, Frank, *Grammar*, Penguin, Harmondsworth, 1982.
Partridge, Eric, *Usage and Abusage*, fifth edition, Penguin, Harmondsworth,
  1981.
Phythian, B. A., *A Concise Dictionary of Correct English*, Hodder and
  Stoughton, London, 1979.
Quirk, Randolph, *The Use of English*, Longmans, London, 1969.
Safire, William, *On Language*, Avon, New York, 1980.
  What's the Good Word?, Times Books, New York, 1982.
Simon, John, *Paradigms Lost: Reflections on Literacy and Its Decline*, Clarkson
  N. Potter, New York, 1980.
Strunk Jr, William, and White, E. B., *The Elements of Style*, third edition,
  Macmillan, New York, 1979.
Wood, Frederick T., *Current English Usage*, Papermac, London, second
  edition, (revised by R. H. and L. M. Flavell), 1981.

Glossary

Grammatical terms are, to quote Frank Palmer, 'largely notional and often extremely vague'. In 'I went swimming', for instance, *swimming* is a present participle; but in 'Swimming is good for you', it is a gerund. Because such distinctions are for many of us a source of continuing perplexity, I have tried to use most such terms sparingly throughout the book. Inevitably, however, they do sometimes appear, and the following is offered as a simple guide for those who are confused or need refreshing. For a fuller discussion, I recommend *A Dictionary of Contemporary American Usage* by Bergen and Cornelia Evans and *A Concise Dictionary of Correct English* by B. A. Phythian.

adjective. A word that qualifies a noun or pronoun: 'a *brick* house', 'a *small* boy', 'a *blue* dress'. Most adjectives have three forms: the positive (*big*), the comparative (*bigger*) and the superlative (*biggest*). Although adjectives are usually easy to recognize when they stand before a noun, they are not always so easily discerned when they appear elsewhere in a sentence, as here: 'He was *deaf*', 'I'm glad to be *alive*', 'She's *awake* now'. Adjectives sometimes function as nouns (the *old*, the *poor*, the *sick*, the *insane*) and sometimes as adverbs (a *bitter*-cold night, a *quick*-witted man). The distinction between an adjective and adverb is often very fine. In 'a great book', *great* is an adjective; but in 'a great many books', it is an adverb.

adverb. A word that qualifies (or describes) any word other than a noun. That may seem a loose definition, but, as Palmer says, the classification is 'quite clearly a "ragbag" or "dustbin", the category into which words that do not seem to belong elsewhere are placed'. In general, adverbs qualify verbs (*badly* played), adjectives (*too* loud) or other adverbs (*very* quickly). As with adjectives, they have the three forms of positive, comparative and superlative (seen respectively in *long*, *longer*, *longest*). A common misconception is the belief that words that end in -ly are always adverbs. *Kindly*, *sickly*, *masterly* and *deadly*, for example, are usually adjectives.

case. The term describes relationships or syntactic functions between parts of speech. A pronoun is in the nominative case (sometimes called the subjective) when it is the subject of a verb ('*He* is here') and in the accusative (sometimes called the objective) when it is the object of a verb or preposition ('Give it to *him*'). Except for six pairs of pronouns (*I/me, he/him, she/her, they/them, we/us* and *who/whom*) and the genitive (which see), English has shed all its case forms.

clause. A group of words that contains a true verb (i.e., a verb functioning as such) and subject. In the sentence 'The house, which was built in 1920, was white' there are two clauses: 'The house was white' and 'which was built in 1920'. The first, which would stand on its own, is called a main or principal or independent clause. The second, which would not stand on its own, is called a dependent or subordinate clause. Sometimes the subject is suppressed in main clauses, as here: 'He got up and went downstairs'. Although 'and went downstairs' would not stand on its own, it is a main clause because the subject has been suppressed. In effect the sentence is saying: 'He got up and he went downstairs'. (See also PHRASE.)

complement. A word or group of words that completes a predicate construction – that is, that provides full sense to the meaning of the verb. In 'He is a rascal', *rascal* is the complement of the verb *is*.

conjunction. A word that links grammatical equivalents, as in 'The President and Prime Minister conferred for two hours' (the conjunction *and* links two nouns) and 'He came yesterday, but he didn't stay long' (the conjunction *but* links two clauses).

genitive. A noun or pronoun is in the genitive case when it expresses possession (*my* house, *his* car, *John's* job). Although some authorities make very small distinctions between genitives and possessives, many others do not. In this book, I have used the term *possessives* throughout.

gerund. A verb made to function as a noun, as with the italicized words here: '*Seeing* is *believing*'; '*Cooking* is an art'; '*Walking* is good exercise'. Gerunds always end in *-ing*.

infinitive. The term describes verbs that are in the infinite mood (that is, that do not have a subject). Put another way, it is a verb form that indicates the action of the verb without inflection to indicate person, number or tense. There are two forms of infinitive: the full (*to go, to see*) and bare (*go, see*), often called simply 'an infinitive without *to*'.

mood. Verbs have four moods:

1. The indicative, which is used to state facts or ask questions (I *am* going; What time *is* it?);

2. The imperative, which indicates commands (*Come* here; *Leave* me alone);

3. The infinite, which makes general statements and has no subject (*To know* her is *to love* her);

4. The subjunctive, which is principally used to indicate hypotheses or suppositions (If I *were* you ...). The uses of the subjunctive are discussed more fully in the body of the book.

noun is usually defined as a word that describes a person, place, thing or quality. Such a definition, as many authorities have noted, is technically inadequate. Most of us would not think of *hope, despair* and *exultation* as things, yet they are nouns. And most of the words that describe qualities – *good, bad, happy* and the like – are not nouns but adjectives. Palmer notes that there is no difference whatever in sense between 'He suffered terribly' and 'His suffering was terrible', yet *suffered* is a verb and *suffering* a noun. There is, in short, no definition for *noun* that isn't circular, though happily for most of us it is one part of speech that is almost always instantly recognizable.

object. Whereas the subject of a sentence tells you who or what is performing an action, the object tells you on whom or on what the action is being performed. In 'I like you', *you* is the object of the verb *like*. In 'They have now built most of the house', *most of the house* is the object of the verb *built*. Sometimes sentences have direct and indirect objects, as here: 'Please send me four tickets'; 'I'll give the dog a bath' (cited by Phythian). The direct objects are *four tickets* and *a bath*. The indirect objects are *me* and *the dog*. Prepositions also have objects. In the sentence 'Give it to him', *him* is the object of the preposition to.

participle. The participle is a verbal adjective. There are two kinds:

present participles, which end in *-ing* (*walking*, *looking*), and past participles, which end in *-d* (*heard*), *-ed* (*learned*), *-n* (*broken*) or *-t* (*bent*). The terms present and past participle can be misleading because present participles are often used in past-tense senses ('They were looking for the money') and past participles are often used when the sense is of the present or future ('He has broken it'; 'Things have never looked better'). When present-tense participles are used to function as nouns, they are called gerunds.

phrase. A group of words that does not have a subject and verb. 'I will come sometime soon' consists of a clause (*I will come*) and phrase (*sometime soon*). Phrases always express incomplete thoughts.

predicate. Everything in a sentence that is not part of the subject (i.e., the verbs, its qualifiers and complements) is called the predicate. In 'The man went to town after work', *The man* is the subject and the rest of the sentence is the predicate. The verb alone is sometimes called the simple predicate.

preposition. A word that connects and specifies the relationship between a noun or noun equivalent and a verb, adjective or other noun or noun equivalent. In 'We climbed over the fence', the preposition *over* connects the verb *climbed* with the noun *fence*. Whether a word is a preposition or conjunction is often a matter of function. In 'The army attacked before the enemy was awake', *before* is a conjunction. But in 'The army attacked before dawn', *before* is a preposition. The distinction is that in the first sentence *before* is followed by a verb. In the second it is not.

pronoun. A word used in place of a noun or nouns. In 'I like walking and reading; such are my pleasures', *such* is a pronoun standing for *reading* and *walking*. Pronouns have been variously grouped by different authorities. Among the more common groupings are personal pronouns (*I*, *me*, *his*, etc.), relative pronouns (*who*, *whom*, *that*, *which*), demonstrative pronouns (*this*, *that*, *these*, *those*) and indefinite pronouns (*some*, *several*, *either*, *neither*, etc.).

subject. The word or phrase in a sentence or clause that indicates who or what is performing the action. In 'I see you', the subject is *I*. In 'Climbing steep hills tires me', *Climbing steep hills* is the subject.

substantive. A word or group of words that performs the function of a noun. In 'Swimming is good for you', *Swimming* is a substantive, as well as a gerund.

verb. Verbs can be defined generally (if a bit loosely) as words that have tense and that denote what someone or something is or does. Verbs that have an object are called transitive verbs – that is, the verb transmits the action from a subject to an object, as in 'He put the book on the table'. Verbs that do not have an object are called intransitive verbs, as in 'He slept all night'; in these the action is confined to the subject.

When it is necessary to indicate more than simple past or present tense, two or more verbs are combined, as in 'I *have thought* about this all week'. Although there is no widely agreed term for such a combination of verbs, I have for convenience followed Fowler in this book and referred to them as compound verbs. The additional or 'helping' verb in such constructions (e.g., *have* in the example above) is called an auxiliary.

MORE ABOUT PENGUINS, PELICANS AND PUFFINS

For further information about books available from Penguins please write to Dept EP, Penguin Books Ltd, Harmondsworth, Middlesex UB7 0DA.

In the U.S.A.: For a complete list of books available from Penguins in the United States write to Dept DG, Penguin Books, 299 Murray Hill Parkway, East Rutherford, New Jersey 07073.

In Canada: For a complete list of books available from Penguins in Canada write to Penguin Books Canada Ltd, 2801 John Street, Markham, Ontario L3R 1B4.

In Australia: For a complete list of books available from Penguins in Australia write to the Marketing Department, Penguin Books Australia Ltd, P.O. Box 257, Ringwood, Victoria 3134.

In New Zealand: For a complete list of books available from Penguins in New Zealand write to the Marketing Department, Penguin Books (N.Z.) Ltd, P.O. Box 4019, Auckland 10.

In India: For a complete list of books available from Penguins in India write to Penguin Overseas Ltd, 706 Eros Apartments, 56 Nehru Place, New Delhi 110019.